Dollars and Sense

Implications of the New Online Technology for Managing the Library

Proceedings of a Conference Program
held in New York City, June 29, 1986

Machine-Assisted Reference Service Section
Reference and Adult Services Division
American Library Association

Bernard F. Pasqualini
editor

American Library Association
Chicago and London   1987

Designed by Marcia Lange

Composed by Prince E. Marshall
in Special Prestige Elite
on a Wang word processor

Printed on 50-pound Glatfelter,
a pH-neutral stock, and
bound in 10-point Carolina
cover stock by
Imperial Printing Company
∞

Contents

Introduction
 Bernard Pasqualini   v

Setting Our Priorities
 Barbara Quint   1

Expanding the Online Search Service
 G. Margaret Porter   9

Pricing Policies and Strategies for Savings
 Martin Kesselman   14

Contract Options for Lowering the Cost of
Online Searching
 James J. Maloney   22

Do User Fees Affect Searcher Behavior?
 Brian Nielsen   29

The Ripple Effect
 Rebecca Kroll   38

Simultaneous Remote Searching
 Verl A. Anderson and Deborah L. Graham   51

Toward Better Online Reference Statistics
 Elizabeth A. Titus   56

Economic Trade-offs of Information Delivery Systems
 John J. Regazzi   72

iv Contents

Frontends and Gateways
      Joseph T. King   76

Full Text Online Delivery
      Delores Meglio   88

What Does It All Mean?
      James H. Sweetland   97

Appendixes

      Funding Methods   105
      Costs and Budgets   111

Contributors   117

Introduction

The papers included in these proceedings are based on a day-long program presented by the Machine-Assisted Reference Section (MARS) of the Reference and Adult Services Division on June 29, 1986, at the annual conference of the American Library Association in New York City. Presented in two half-day sessions, the program attempted to take the online user and manager from the basics of financial management through the effects of new technology on online services.

The committee working on this program used the MARS Cost and Finance Committee's Budgeting and Finance outlines as the framework for the program. Those outlines and bibliographies are included in the addendum. The program committee issued a call for papers to professionals working in the field asking for contributions that would identify new trends and services in online information retrieval that impact the cost and/or funding of such services in libraries.

Major themes and specific topics to be covered in the program were:

> Direct cost elements of online searching (online charges, communications, etc.);
> Indirect cost elements of online searching (hardware, documentation, training, operating costs, etc.);
> Creative approaches to funding (short and long-term);
> Economics of enduser systems and grant funding;

Choosing vendor services/databases, gateways,
contract options, and front end software;
Cost-effectiveness of micros for searching, impact
of higher telecommunication speeds and service
options, impact on document delivery (online
service, print, ILL), and planning for
equipment maintenance, replacement, and
acquisition;
Use of online for ready reference, costs and
consequences of promotion, significance of
changing vendor pricing structures;
Administering an online service (statistics,
recordkeeping, allocation of funds.

The committee was gratified by the number of responses it received--enough to conduct a second program of
equal length without diminishing the quality. The papers
chosen were those we felt transmitted the greatest amount
of information to the widest audience. Each of the speakers brought differing viewpoints and levels of experience
to the program all are committed to achieving excellence
in online service.

The choices for the keynote and wrap-up speakers
were extremely important, as those speakers needed to tie
together a diverse group of papers on a large range of
topics. The committee's choices could not have been
better: Barbara Quint, editor of Database End-User, was
able at an early hour to rouse the crowd with a stirring
speech; and James Sweetland of the School of Library and
Information Science, University of Wisconsin-Milwaukee,
was able to neatly tie the program up. The final part of
the program, which is not reproduced in these proceedings,
was a Vendor Showcase in which four vendors presented new
or upcoming products that would have an impact on online
services.

The intent of this program was to widen the vision
of librarians, information specialists, managers, and
library administrators concerning online services in their
libraries. Perhaps Barbara Quint summed it up best when
she said, "Database technology can convert any library,
any library system, from an archive, a collection of pos-
sibilities, into an answer machine pushing beyond the
information needs of any existing user community. ... Too
many libraries continue to operate as if online were an
exotic and optional supplement to traditional library
service. It is not. It is better. It is more comprehensive. It has more scope. And it is cheaper."

   As in any undertaking, there are many people to
thank. I would like to thank all of the presenters. I
would also like to thank the members of the MARS Program
Committee who worked so hard: Janet Bruman, Co-Chair,
Pamela Sieving, Mary Hardin, Emelie Shroder, Kathleen
Kluegel, and Maria Soule.
   I would also like to thank James Maloney, Rebecca
Whitaker, Nancy Green-Maloney, and Andrew Hansen for their
support and assistance. Special appreciation is due Prince
E. Marshall for his help during the word processing stage
of this publication.

Bernard F. Pasqualini

Setting Our Priorities

Barbara Quint

Online databases are a superior form of information
technology offering major breakthroughs for access across
the full range of individual and social information needs.
So what else is new? There's not an aware librarian who
doesn't know that fact and hasn't known it for years.
Database technology can convert any library or, any
library system from an archive--a collection of possi-
bilities--into an answer machine pushing beyond the information needs of any existing user community. Our clients
do not know all that they could know. They do not know
enough to ask for all that we could do for them. So what
else is new? Every aware public service librarian has
known for years that the new technologies offer the potential for revolutionary redesign of library services.
In reference and public service library work, online
is the technology of preference. It is faster. It is more
powerful. It has greater scope. And, measured in value
delivered, it is cheaper. Naturally it is cheaper for
tasks that are impossible to do by hand, but it is also
faster and cheaper for things that can be done by hand.
It even enhances existing investment by enabling you to
tap the deposits of earlier technologies through massive
bibliographic databases, as well as providing new answer
resources with files existing in no other mode. What else
is new?
What else is new is not enough, not by a long
shot. Too many libraries continue to operate as if online
were an exotic and optional supplement to traditional
library service. It is not. It is better. It is more
comprehensive. It has more scope. And it is cheaper.

How in God's name could that be interpreted as optional?
Online database technology is superior, and I include the
full range-traditional mainframe dial-up or hardwired
connections into central computers, nontraditional mainframe with hook-ups via FM radio transmissions or satel-
lites transmitting directly to local microcomputers, new
localized databases (magnetic, like floppies), Bernoulli
boxes, and hard disks, or optical disks (like CD-ROM),
interactive compact disks, laser disks, and interactive
videodiscs. All online databases are superior by any
reasonable standard measuring delivery of information.

Why has the potential for radical redesign of libraries and their services not happened? Money. That's
what everybody says, but I wonder. I would like to challenge that it is money. Money follows priorities. Money
is a decision to commit resources made by people--people
in institutions, people in professions, people as individuals, people in societies.

May I suggest that if we reexamine our budget
priorities we will discover that a radical change is in
order if we judge our expenditures against the delivery of
information. Sunset budgeting techniques will allow you
to take a look at your operating budget, not in comparison
with what your totals were last year, but with what your
goals are. Ultimately, that kind of budgeting approach is
necessary because, when all is said and done, there are
only two kinds of money--new money and old money. New
money is what you get from someone who has never given any
to you before, or it's money from old sources but more
than you've ever gotten from them before. Old money is
somebody else's money. New money is carrot money, elic-
ited with promises of benefits warranting major new investment. We have tried getting it for years with varying
levels of ingenuity and with limited success. Old money,
rerouted money, is stick money. It tells the people getting the money now that they're going to suffer because
you need their cash, that you've got better things to do
with their money than what they're doing with it. A joint
carrot-and-stick approach, by the way, is probably the
best strategy, because without a stick you don't get many
carrots in this world.

Reexamining budget priorities will be a painful
process, but it cannot be more painful for professionals
than knowing about the deprivation that our clients and
customers have borne over the years since online technology was developed. They have not gotten the best we
had to give. Most of them have not gotten anything from

the new technology because we have not been able to break
through this barrier. The time has come to ask some hard
questions about budgets across the full range of library
functions--questions leaving nobody's ox ungored.

What are the people in technical services doing
with our money? Will somebody explain to me why monographs are so bloody important in a library's collection?
Will somebody explain to me why that skimpy bit of data
that the technical services staff puts out for the customer should absorb so much of a library's resources? Will
somebody explain to me why this group of database builders
seems to operate on the theory that not only should every
title have an indexer but also every copy? Why should
every library assign professional staff slots to cataloging? When the goal of catalogers is so often to make
each library come out with substantially the same thing,
why not have one person catalog and everybody else download? That way it always comes out the same. Why don't
all libraries network their cataloging?

Will somebody tell me why they are assigning
professional staff to do descriptive cataloging or even
the assignment of call numbers? These systems, these
databases that they're building, are supposed to be used
by customers off the street. Are you telling me that
library clerical staff can't manipulate the system suf-
ficiently to locate items but people off the street are
expected to operate it? Let clerical staff tap the bibliographic networks--OCLC, RLIN, whatever. Let them find
the references, download the references, and create the
catalog. And give us the money!

If technical services won't give us their money, if
they want to hold on to it, they're going to have to earn
it with something better than a mechanized replication of
19th century access tools. If they think library col-
lections are so important, then why are they covering only
monographs? That's a narrow portion of any library's
collection--in an academic library, a very narrow portion. If they want to keep that money, I want every piece
of material in the collection accessible and that includes
periodical holdings. And by periodical holdings, I include the full references for all the articles within
those periodicals. I want it all. If you want to know
where to get all that data, I have a suggestion. Just
pick up your budgets and trot over to database producers
with cover-to-cover indexing of major periodicals. If you
belong to an academic library take your list of periodi-

cals to the Institute for Scientific Information (ISI).
Match it against their monster citation indexes--<u>Science
Citation Index,</u> <u>Arts and Humanities Citation Index,</u>
<u>Social Science Citation Index</u>--and you won't come back
with very many unmatched. Download the references. Buy a
tape. Cut a deal. If you belong to a public library,
take your list to Information Access Company (IAC)--pro-
ducers of <u>Magazine Index</u>, <u>Legal Resources Index</u>, <u>Trade and
Industry Index</u>, <u>Management Contents</u>, <u>National Newspaper
Index</u>, et al.--or try <u>Wilsonline</u>. Buy a tape, download,
buy a CD-ROM, buy a laser disk, buy whatever you need.

But when a customer comes in and asks "Do you have
something on . . . . ?", that catalog should answer the
question fully. If technical services is willing to
develop full collection-access databases, we'll let them
keep the money. Public service may save a certain amount
of money when online public access catalogs siphon off all
the database searches reference librarians make to simply
tap their own holdings, all the times they go into indexes
simply to find out what their libraries have in the building, already paid for and sitting on a shelf. With the
full collection covered, the online catalog would qualify
as a major breakthrough in a library's power to inform.
Without it, those technical service budgets should be in
trouble.

Next, library administration. What's all this
chatter about building funds? Why all these plans for
branch libraries? Let's look at branch libraries. First
you've got to buy the corner, then the building, then a
collection to put in the building, all of which is repeated in the central library. Why don't you just buy yourself a really good online information system, a good control system for what is in the central library? Central
will always have much more than any branch. Add online
outlets for every home in the city. Link the whole town
through the cable television system, for example. Put
terminals in public facilities. Assign special numbers
for businesses. Give a password to everybody who has a
microcomputer with a modem. Attach an online ordering
module to the information system. Buy a motor scooter
with a basket, a bookmobile for the heavier stuff, and--
presto!--branch libraries. You could get a much better
information delivery system for your money than building
funds.

Before I hear your protests about shortage of
funds, let me tell you something about my background. I

come from the Rand Corporation. We have 27 search services accessing close to 900 databases. It seems that whenever I tell my academic and public library friends and colleagues about Rand and all its databases, I listen to a tale of woe ending with "It must be wonderful to work in a place like that. I wish I worked at a rich library like you do." But when I look at them, they all look like bank tellers they're so well dressed. The soles of their shoes have never touched anything but textile. God forbid they should walk into a workplace and have the colors of the drapes and the chairs not match. God forbid they should walk across a parking lot and not have the plant life evenly aligned at assorted eye levels. Poor? What matters most in the information facility? Decor or databases? Decor their libraries have, facilities they have, buildings they have and can get more, but online databases their administration treats as an expensive frill. I work at the Rand library. We walk on linoleum! We have no drapes. Our basement windows are spotted from the sprinkler. If we chin ourselves from those windows, we get to see dirt. But we've got databases!

Gunfighters in the old west had a saying, if you watch their hands, you're dead; watch their eyes. If you listen to the words of administration about why they spend money the way they do, you'll spend your working life in Boot Hill. Watch the money, where it goes and where it flows. That's where the priorities are. The fact is that libraries have a particular problem. Our clients are our bosses. Our clients are our audiences. The people who decide how much money we get and how well we do our jobs are not people who know how to do the job. So you find people investing in libraries as a kind of romantic, mythic land of their youth. That's why you get plenty of money for gift stamps for books, but when you try to get the memorial online terminal, you're in big trouble. Somehow getting a search service bill mailed to you each month lacks the cachet of a permanent structure.

Are we finished with library administration? What about public service people? We're all sinners here. How many people here get Mead--Lexis or Nexis? That's too few. How many get Dialog? Happy Dialog! Are all of you aware that Dialog carries full-text sources? Very good. Are all of you aware that there are some 130 or so in the ASAP files, maybe another 5 or 6 in the new McGraw Hill file, plus major reference sources--the Encyclopedia of Associations and such? Very, very good. How many of

those titles of full text sources are included in your
library's catalog or list of serial holdings? How many of
you here can recite those titles in alphabetic order?
Well, if you can't, how do you expect your customers to?
Do you expect them to know more than the professionals?
How many of you have erected obstacle courses that customers have to cross to get an online search? Hippity
hop, hippity hop, two turns to the left, one to the right.
It's like trying to get an address out of an information
operator. And why are we doing that? We're controlling
costs instead of answering information needs. The more
ornate the design of the obstacle course, the better the
chance that we'll forget that it is still a barrier instead
of a gateway. The public does not know more than professionals. They shouldn't be expected to.

The new technology has reached critical mass. It
is breakthrough technology, revolutionary in impact.
There's one very good side to using such a technology.
Breakthrough technology has to do one thing that ordinary
technological advances don't. It has to prove that it can
do everything the technologies that preceded it did and
more. That's why with breakthrough technologies you so
often have to take money from people who were spending it
another way. Ultimately you have to realign expectation
and realign resources. You have to educate people. To do
this, you have to be able to deliver a certain critical
mass. Why were there so few hands when I asked about Mead
Data Central? Because Mead costs big bucks. Why has Mead
succeeded so well financially? In part because it went
past us, directly to the end-user community. In part
because when it got there, it delivered the goods. The
online systems that we have now, not just Mead, are very
capable of delivering the goods, particularly with the
end-user interfaces and end-user routes that are in development and in place. They can set up critical mass. They
can deliver the goods, day after day, question after question. They do not need constant coaching from professionals. They need some coaching. They need some support,
but they do not need constant propping up by expert humans
doing everything for everybody. They are now at that
point where what they need is the plug into the wall con-
nected to the money and the customers. And if we don't
provide it, somebody else will.

There are windows of opportunity in technology.
Unless my tongue slipped, there is one phrase that I
haven't used. I have not referred to online databases as

a new technology. It isn't new. It's over 20 years old.
That window of opportunity for the library profession has
been open for 20 to 25 years. In my opinion, it will not
be open 20 years from now. If we don't move fast, somebody else will do the job. As long as the job gets done,
why should we care whether we're the ones who do it?
Well, we have legitimate self-interest involved. That's a
reason to care. What will future libraries be after somebody else starts providing database access? The small
ones will be the lucky ones. They will provide testing
rooms for technology. Come in and sample. See a CD-ROM
before you buy your own. Try out a database, try out a
gateway before you go home and subscribe. These libraries
will be the lucky ones. At least they'll get to see the
world as it goes by. Large libraries, on the other hand,
will be warehouses, depots where everything the advancing
full-text technologies have not creamed off is stored.
Some will serve as social welfare agencies with a rather
odd view of appropriate decor for the homeless. And of
course they will remain sentimental relics of an earlier
era, places where people go to share a sense of history by
touching the book, a deposit of 16th century information
technology, to get that mythic feeling and then go home or
to the office to do serious information work. And what
about the librarian? The brightest among us will disclaim
all identity as a librarian. We'll be working in the
information industry doing good work, active work, sup-
plying the goods. We will not wish it to be known that we
ever considered a career as an anachronism. For those of
us left in libraries, the less informed of our customers
in that future age will see us as a rather beloved anachronisms. The smarter among them will see us as somewhat
less than beloved anachronisms, since we will be highly
priced. Those who do not see us as such, those who are
too ignorant to know exactly how far behind in technology
we are, we will not only have professionally failed, we
will also have betrayed.

    In the larger picture, who cares as long as cust-
omers get what they need? So what if we're not the ones
to provide it? I think it does make a difference whether
it's us, because only the people in our profession--
information professionals, informationists, librarians,
whatever you want to call us--will do it as it should be
done. We're the only people who have and always have had
the knowledge that information is an extremely intimate
product, that information is just data until you see the

gleam in their eyes. The tool people don't have it. The
industry people don't have it. The customers who don't
know how information reaches them or doesn't reach them
don't have it. They don't know how and when information
becomes knowledge. As generalists, we are prepared to
carry on an educational, a critical function. For an
information industry person, no matter how good, once the
sale is made, the sale is made. We're the ones who will
stay behind after class to talk about the bigger picture.
To point out that not only did the encounter with the
database find today's data but it also taught clients a
technique that will answer the assignments of all their
tomorrows. We will show them that databases form the
building blocks of a system that can synthesize information from many different worlds to create a new information environment and to produce a new kind of information consumer. This is something we can do. If we don't
do it, then it won't be done.

     To tell you the truth, we should not be discussing
this topic now. If things were going as they should,
other topics would be on our agenda. Two occur to me. One
is how to integrate new technologies that manufacture
information--micros, for example--with the technologies
for storing large amounts of outside information. That
would be a marvelous topic, but who is ready yet? We
could also be discussing what should be the issue of the
1980s--quality of data, synthesizing data. All of this
data pouring in from multiple sources has got to be compared, evaluated, integrated. Librarians can perform a
critical function there. But we still haven't got the car
in first gear, we're still in the solenoid era.

     There's not much time left, no time for being metic-
ulous, no time for doing it perfectly. We're so wrong now
that anything must be better than this. There is no time
for being patient. Patience is an excuse for inaction.
There is no time to be tolerant of people hanging onto our
money for vain, outmoded purposes of their own or self-
serving aggrandizement. And there's no time to be polite.
We've got to get this thing going. The window is closing
I would like to suggest that all of us--professionals,
administrators, money people, whomever--stop frittering
around!

Expanding the Online Search Service:
Common Sense and Cost Considerations

G. Margaret Porter

Online professionals are constantly receiving information on new databases, systems, and technology through the mail and the professional literature, as well as through requests from patrons for access to online resources. In her column "Online Databases" in Library Journal (April 1, 1986), Carol Tenopir states that since 1979 there has been a 30-40% growth in the number of publicly available databases, and one directory of online sources currently lists over 440 online vendors as opposed to 59 in 1979. Full-text databases and optical disc technology such as CD-ROM pose additional challenges.

In view of this rapid growth and the attention that online databases are getting in print media outside the library literature, it is inevitable that a search service has to expand to keep up with new developments and to respond to increased demands. However, limited resources make it important to avoid a haphazard approach to expansion. Most of us by combining common sense and professional expertise can judge whether or not expanding the service is the logical or right approach at any given time, but we have to be able to clearly justify our decisions to patrons as well as to supervisors and/or administrators.

There is currently very little in the literature that provides guidelines or even a checklist of what to take into consideration. I will therefore attempt to provide some guidelines. Two groups of factors will be discussed in this paper: common sense factors and actual cost factors. Each area influences the other and, since every search service is different, all factors may not be applicable, but some of these factors should be considered to prevent costly and/or unnecessary growth. The first area to be considered is common sense factors. Consider expansion in light of these factors:

    1. Clientele served. Look at the clientele the search service serves and determine what their primary needs are. Do they need research in specific subjects or fields, brief factual information, statistical data rather than bibliographic information, etc.? Are the patrons a highly specialized homogenous group or do they consist of a varied clientele with various needs at different levels of sophistication? Then, of course, examine the proposed addition to the search service to determine whether it fits the needs of clientele.

    2. Anticipated usage. Will there be too few users of the system? Is the information provided too special-ized to be used across the board? Does it meet the re-search needs of only one or two faculty members, for ex-ample. Is a new system being considered primarily because of one or two files or databases? If this is the case might these be available on another system already ac-cessed within the institution?

    3. External resources. Investigate the resources available externally such as other libraries, businesses, networks, users groups, and cooperative library agencies. Try to work out some reciprocal agreements with other agen-cies in your area for searching. If no local users group is established, this may be a good time to do so. A direc-tory of local online capabilities is a useful product to come out of a users group.

    4. Volume of searching. Look at the volume of searching already being done. If the volume is low, is it because not enough access is being provided? If this is the case then expansion is desirable. If the volume is low because there is no great demand or need for online searching, then an effort should be made to generate interest in what is already available.

    5. Staff and equipment. If the volume is already high, project the implications of adding another system in terms of staff time for training and actual searching as well as equipment needs. This factor has real influence on actual cost considerations.

    6. Availability of source documents. If a biblio-graphic system that is not available full-text is being considered look at the availability of source documents locally and through document delivery services.

    7. Political implications. Finally, because we

all function in the "real" world, rather than in an ideal
one, what are the political realities? If there is a
request from the provost's office or from a high level
executive or administrator the responses we come up with
to these common sense considerations may be immaterial.
Real costs or dollar figures may in the end be immaterial
as well, but they nevertheless tend to have more impact on
decision making.

The following considerations, then, are cost considerations.

1. Sign-up costs. Within this category look for
the up-front subscription charge. This may be a one time
charge or an annual one. Are sign-up costs and/or charges
dependent on the number of passwords? Is there a prepayment plan available or necessary? Will prepayment
lower the online charges? Is there a minimum monthly
charge independent of usage?

2. Search and citation costs. Even within a search
service that is fee-based the online charges are of consequence. Even the most experienced searchers make errors
for which the patron will not be charged. Training and
practice time may be even more important on expensive
systems or databases.

3. Documentation costs. Is there a charge for
file, database, or system documentation? If some documentation is provided free, will there be enough information available to allow for efficient searching, or will
it be necessary to purchase additional documentation?
Also, at this point determine how many sets of documentation will be needed.

4. Training costs. What kind of training is provided and at what cost? Take into consideration the location for training. How much travel will be involved? If
formal training is not available or is too costly can online time be allocated from the vendor at reduced cost?
If this option is not available determine what is a feasible allocation of online training time per searcher. At
this time it is also wise to look at who should be trained
Would it be more cost effective to train only one searcher
for the system or does the anticipated usage require several searchers to be trained? The question of how many and
whom to train should be thought of in terms of the next
point.

5. Efficiency of searchers. Will the efficiency
of searchers be affected by adding another system protocol? How different is the protocol from others already

mastered? This is a "hidden" cost factor not easily measured in dollars, but it should nevertheless be taken into
consideration. The number of systems an intermediary can
use effectively varies before he or she reaches the point
of diminishing returns, both in terms of learning a new
skill and the effect additional protocols may have on the
efficiency of searching those already acquired. Vague as
this cost may be, it is an area that needs to be looked at.

6. <u>Substitution</u>. Substitution as a cost saving
factor should be considered. Would it make sense to substitute a new or additional system for one already accessed? Look at how already accessed systems are being
used and at how much they are costing the library and/or
the patrons. In an area that is expanding and changing as
rapidly as online searching, discontinuing "old" systems
and adding new ones may be the most cost effective way of
expanding. Much has been said about cancelling print indexes in favor of online access. This may be a cost saving factor, but should be looked at closely, taking into
consideration the training of additional staff, citation
charges for online printing, and equipment needs and usage.

7. <u>Impact on interlibrary loan</u>. As mentioned
earlier, availability of source documents should be considered when evaluating a database or system. What are
the implications for interlibrary loan in terms of staff
time and costs? If a document delivery system is available, what are those costs and who should pay--the library
or the patron?

Finally, after all or some of these questions and
considerations have been looked at, the ultimate question
to be answered is: Will this improve or enhance the service already provided?

Bibliography

Dowd, Sheila, John H. Whaley Jr., Marcia Pankake.
    "Reactions to 'Funding Online Services from the
    Materials Budget,'" <u>College and Research
    Libraries</u> (May 1986): 230-237.
Ewbank, W. B. "Comparison Guide to Selection of Databases
    and Database Services," <u>Drexel Library Quarterly</u>
    (Summer-Fall 1982): 189-204.
Haar, John M. "The Politics of Information: Libraries and
    Online Retrieval Systems," <u>Library Journal</u> (Feb.
    1, 1986): 40-43.
Herther, Nancy K. "CD ROM Technology: a New Era for
    Information Storage and Retrieval? <u>Online</u> (November
    1985): 17-28.

Hildreth, Charles R. "Communicating with Online Catalogs and Other Retrieval Systems: The Need for a Standard Command Language" Library Hi Tech (Issue 13, 1986): 7-11.

Nichol, K. M. "Database Proliferation: Implications for Librarians," Special Libraries (April 1983): 110-118.

Poole, Jay M. "Funding Online Services from the Materials Budget" College and Research Libraries (May 1986): 225-229.

Tenopir, Carol. "Change or Crisis in the Database Industry?" Library Journal (April 1, 1986): 46-47.

Pricing Policies and
Strategies for Savings

Martin Kesselman

Pricing policies vary greatly from one online service to another. Most pricing policies are based on connect hour charges which are variable and tend to be biased towards those users with high speed modems, those searching with microcomputers who can setup their strategies offline and upload them to the search system, or those searchers with a great deal of training and experience. The big advantage of connect-time charges is that they can be useful in predicting how much a search will cost. Ideally, however, pricing should reflect the volume of information obtained from an online search and not be limited to connect hour charges alone. With minimal connect hour charges, searchers would be encouraged to browse and interact more with the online search service. But, as data transmission speeds increase, resulting in lower connect charges, database producers and vendors will increasingly be forced to utilize charging methods not based on connect time.

Some online vendors are already offering new pricing schemes such as increased royalties for online and offline printing, charging for the actual work done by the computer for various searches and charging by fixed costs. With the new pricing algorithm for the National Library of Medicine (NLM) search service, most charges are now based on the actual work, or central processing units (CPU) carried out by the online system's computer. NLM's pricing now includes low online connect charges but it has

added charges based on the number of characters printed,
the number of disk accesses (for a computer resource
charge), the number of carriage returns and search statements, and the number of citations printed. Charges are
also higher during peak usage times. The Chemical
Abstracts Service's CAS Online charging mechanism also
consists of low online connect costs and print charges
with added search fees for various system capabilities.
For example, search fees can be as much as $75 for a
chemical structure search which requires a great deal of
CPU. But, for academic libraries, CAS offers a special
account that can be used evenings and weekends for only
10% of the daytime fees.

An alternative pricing scheme may entail a fixed
cost-per-search or a subscription plan for unlimited
access. Search Helper, used for searching Information
Access Company (IAC) files such as Magazine Index on
Dialog, and Wilsearch, used for accessing Wilsonline
databases, offer opportunities for low fixed-cost searching. With a maximum number of subscriptions, costs can be
as low as $2.50 per search on Search Helper or $1 per
search with Wilsearch. Databases are also being offered
on a subscription basis at fixed costs in CD-ROM and other
laser disk formats. These databases can then be searched
as much as desired in-house without the meter running.
Database producers are still experimenting with pricing
for these new formats. Development costs for these
services are not that great if the information to be en-
coded is already in machine readable form. However, the
upfront production costs are high. Laser disks may provide more revenue for database producers as they may eliminate the online vendor as a middleman. But database
producers still need to decide how to price these new
formats in relation to comparable print and online products, not fully knowing the effect, if any, CD-ROM may
have on print subscriptions or online usage. With print
subscriptions, libraries may keep back issues if they
cancel the subscription at a later date. This is not the
case with the majority of laser disk products announced so
far.

One way to save money is to do your searches during
evenings and weekends and obtain accounts with Bibliographic Retrieval Service's BRS After Dark and Dialog's
Knowledge Index, both of which offer substantial savings
over daytime services. During the day, BRS's Colleague
and Brkthru services are also lower cost alternatives. If

you are teaching classes how to do online searching, Dialog offers a classroom instruction plan and BRS offers an
instructor password at just $15 per hour. And if you're
willing to experiment, you may be able, just for the cost
of a telephone call, to make use of the many free databases or bulletin board services available, such as the
ones offered by the U.S. Naval Observatory, the handi-
capped Educational Exchange, the Alternative Fuel Data
Bank, and others.

There may also be cases in which the costs of
accessing databases through European online search
services may be lower than searching a database on one of
the U.S. services. Especially for databases in the
biosciences and health, the nonprofit DIMDI search service
based in West Germany offers low connect-hour and print
charges, and the London-based Data-Star offers a special
academic discount. However, telecommunications costs to
Europe are significantly higher and may require opening up
an international telecommunications account with additional monthly account maintenance fees. Determine if European
access is worthwhile for the databases you search most
often. European services may also be more cost-effective
during periods when the U.S. dollar is stronger on world
markets.

Because a significant amount of search cost is
still based on connect time, below are some suggested
cost-effective strategies and techniques to use when
formulating and inputting your searches. They will not
only save online time and money, but may be more relevant
for your client.

For telecommunications--unless you search very
rarely--use a 1200 baud modem for faster searching and
significant savings in the costs of online printing. If
you are buying a modem now, you might consider a 2400 baud
modem as access at this speed is already available in some
parts of the country. You'll also get faster response if
you don't search during periods of peak usage. On the
East Coast, for example, it's best to search early in the
morning before the West Coast comes online. As to which
service is fastest, a study published in the April 1986
issue of Database compared the four major networks in
different time periods and geographic locations. The
study found that Dialnet, at $6 per hour, was not only the
cheapest but the fastest as well, followed by Tymnet,
Uninet, and Telenet.

Great savings in connect time can also be realized
by searching with a microcomputer and various

communications and front-end software packages. These
packages allow the searcher to input a search before going
online, edit search statements before they're sent, and
type ahead the next search line while waiting for the
response from the previous statement. These capabilities
are especially attractive to those of us who are not fast
typists and they also provide the opportunity to correct
spelling errors and edit search statements before they're
uploaded to the online service. These packages also allow
you to print online into a buffer at full communications
speed and save your search strategies offline on disk for
later use, thus saving the costs for permanent storage on
the online service.

     Good search strategy preparation and planning is
also important. Rather than being flustered online with
the meter running, try to do your search preparation
offline and think of various contingency plans or of how
you might deal with too many or too few postings. If at
all possible, try to have the patron present during the
search, and conduct an effective presearch interview which
will help keep the search focused and well-defined and the
costs low. Because they are more specific and will only
retrieve highly relevant citations, searches of greater
precision can usually be done at lower costs than searches
requiring high recall, in which many synonyms for each
concept must be searched and many free-text terms used.
It might be preferable, especially with a complicated
search statement, to write it out first and see if it
makes sense, so you don't miss important punctuation when
you input the strategy online. If you do get into a snag
online, go offline to reconsider your search strategy. To
help with this, logoff hold on Dialog and ..off continue
on BRS will sign you off but will for a brief period of
time place a bookmark in the database you're searching and
at the point you signed off. When you sign back on,
you'll be reconnected at just the point you left off. In
case you don't sign back on in time, save your search
temporarily as a precaution. Also, remember that online
is not always the way to go. There are cases in which it
may be faster or more cost-effective to answer the query
using a print source, such as when an index includes the
subject heading you're most interested in as well as a
relevant subheading.

     A knowledge of database indexing policies can lead
to improved search precision and recall and can also save
search time and costs. Try to use controlled vocabulary

terms; you will then not need to search for many synonyms for a concept of interest. And use a precoordinated subject heading, if one is available, such as Pregnancy in Diabetes on <u>Medline</u> rather than searching each concept separately. Some databases such as the U. S. Department of Energy's <u>DOE Energy</u> employ upposting with their indexing so that a searcher need only select a broad term in order to also retrieve items indexed under more specific headings. Several databases make use of codes such as the SIC (standard industrial classification) codes or registry numbers for chemical compounds. The codes are controlled, so you need not search for synonyms. <u>Medline</u> includes numbered hierarchical trees for families of related subject headings and the searcher can truncate these tree numbers to the level of specificity desired. For example, if a searcher is interested in articles on all liver diseases, truncating or exploding the tree number for liver diseases will also pick up articles on specific liver diseases such as hepatitis without the searcher having to type in each term separately. On other databases, where codes are used for broad concepts, you can focus your search on a particular subject area without having to type in an exhaustive list of keywords. On some services such as Dialog, if you're interested in a group of codes, you can select them by ranges rather than by typing in each code separately.

In comparing features of various online vendors, besides looking at price, look at other value-added features that will save money. It's often difficult to compare the costs of searching a database on one online service to the costs of searching it on another because databases are updated and processed differently. For the same search, online services may come up with differing results. A better comparison would be to compare the costs per relevant citation obtained. Look instead for those features that may save you money for the particular search you're working on. For example, you may be able to limit by language easily on a particular database on one vendor and not another. Also, some online services may have large databases all in one file or in several file segments by time periods. If you're only interested in current information, it is cheaper to search the segmented file. If you're interested in a comprehensive retrospective search, using the combined file will avoid having to save and execute the search in the other file segments.

Some cost-effective features available on most

online services are limiting, nesting, truncation, expanding, and command stacking. Limit capabilities can be used
to quickly focus your search to certain parameters such as
year, language, or major concept. On Dialog, if you know
in advance that you wish to limit a search you can use
limitall for much faster processing and lower costs. Nesting allows the searcher to perform several search operations in one search statement and can be used for distri-
buted proximity searching. Truncation can be used for
retrieving singular and plural forms of a word or those
words with the same root. In many cases, however, rather
than choosing unlimited truncation, it may be preferable
to expand. Expand, or neighbor, or root, as it is called
on some services, enables the searcher to see all available alphabetical variations of a term or name. Any varia-
tion can then be chosen selectively. With expand you need
not be overly concerned with spelling and punctuation and
you immediately know the postings for each term displayed. With command stacking you can type several search
statements at once. After you press the carriage return,
the statements are then executed in order, one at a time,
at high speed. Command stacking is especially useful in
multifile searching when you are saving and executing a
search strategy, and when you already know the results of
a search, for example, in a preliminary search on Dialog's
Dialindex or BRS's CROS database.
When you are doing multifile searching, start with
the cheapest file first for inputting and adjusting your
search. Some online services have edit commands allowing
you to cleanup your search strategy before saving it and
executing it on other files. With multifile searching,
try to integrate terms from the various databases you wish
to search into a master strategy that can be executed
across files of interest. When you are inputting your
search for the first time, if you don't have a micro, you
can choose the default file or better yet, databases with
free time, to stack commands for a preliminary search
before going into another file. When you are doing cross-
file searching in a few related databases such as Medline
and Health Planning, or ERIC and ECER, it is possible to
eliminate duplicates, thus saving unnecessary printing
costs. Hedges are special kinds of search strategies that
you might permanently save online or store on disk and
then execute as needed. Hedges usually represent a concept, such as an age group, that you find yourself using
over and over in your searches. Some database producers

such as Compendex and PsycInfo make the hedges they have
produced available for general use. Check in database
user aids for these hedges. In the case of PsycInfo you
can get a listing of hedges stored on Dialog by typing
?Psycsave.
        Printing options also offer opportunities for
savings. Especially in ready reference situations, if your
library owns the printed database equivalent, you may be
able to just print the title and abstract number as a free
format. The patron can then look up the abstract numbers
in the print source to obtain the complete citations for
titles that are of interest. The prices for each format
can be determined online on Dialog by typing ?rates followed by the file number. On many files in which only
selected documents contain abstracts, you may be able to
print documents with abstracts in full format and documents without abstracts in a citation format, thus saving
the costs for printing all items in full format. Also,
don't forget to compare the charges for online versus
offline printing which may vary dramatically from one file
to the next. Depending on the database, printing online
at 1200 baud is often cheaper than printing offline, with
the added benefit of obtaining immediate results. however, as searching with micros becomes the norm, many
producers may charge more for online printing, assuming
that you may be downloading and potentially reusing the
citations from the downloaded search.
        Finally, don't forget to make use of database user
aids, which usually include many examples of cost-saving
measures. And feel free to call database producers' and
vendors' toll-free numbers for assistance in setting-up
more cost-effective search strategies.

Bibliography

Baiget, T., "Prices and Online Searching: The Cheapest
    Host Is Not Always the One You Think." Proceedings
    of the Sixth International Online Information
    Meeting, 1982: 27-37.
Bourne, Charles P., "Online Systems: History, Technology
    and Economics. "Journal of the American Society
    for Information Science, 31(3): 155-160 (May 1980).
Boyle, Harry F., "The Pricing of Information—A Search
    Based Approach to Pricing an Online Search
    Service." Online Review, 6(6): 517-523 (December
    1982).

"International Comparative Price Guide to Databases
    Online." Online Review (February and August 1986).
Kenton, David, "The Development of a More Equitable
    Method of Billing for Online Services." Online,
    8(5): 13-17 (September 1984).
Koch, Jean E., "A Review of the Costs and
    Cost-Effectiveness of Online Bibliographic
    Searching." RSR, 10(1): 59-64 (Spring 1982).
Lesko, Matthew, "Low-Cost On-Line Databases." Byte,
    10(10): 167-174 (October 1984).
Pemberton, Jeff, "The Inverted File: Some Observations on
    the Pricing of Online Services." Online, 8(4): 6-7
    (July 1984).
Saffady, William, "Availability and Cost of Online Search
    Services." Library Technology Reports, 21: 1-97
    (January-February 1985).
Scott, Ralph Lee, "Communications Costs for Database
    Access--Waiting is Costly." Database, 9(2):
    110-115 (April 1986).
Tenopir, Carol, "Online Databases: Pricing Policies."
    Library Journal, 109(12): 1300-1301 (July 1984).
Zais-Gabbert, Harriet and Roderer, Nancy K., "The Role of
    Evaluation in Pricing: Database Producers'
    Perspective." Proceedings of the National Online
    Meeting, 1981: 539-547.

Contract Options for Lowering the Cost of Online Searching

James J. Maloney

One of the most useful aspects of a "Consumer Reports" evaluation of a product is the checklist of features that enables people to ask the right questions about the product or service. This paper offers a checklist to use in selecting or reviewing the discount and contract options offered by online search services. The options of seven widely used services were reviewed for purposes of this paper:

>Bibliographic Retrieval Services (BRS)
>Dialog Information Services
>Mead Data Central's Lexis and Nexis (Mead)
>Pergamon Infoline Services
>Systems Development Corporation (SDC)
>Scientific and Technical Information Network (STN)
>The H. W. Wilson Company's Wilsonline

THE PRICING OF ONLINE SERVICES

The most elemental method of setting a price is known as "cost-plus pricing," in which a standard mark-up is added to the cost of the product. Mainframe-computer time-sharing services price the simultaneous use of their computers by the hour or fraction thereof. But overhead

in the "cost" portion of the product, originally limited
to CPU time, grew as investment in customer support services grew.

The price for the use of the computer is still
commonly expressed among online information services as
either a charge per search or as a charge per connect
hour. The charges are not mutually exclusive in some
services. However, the connect-hour charge is common to
all services.

Telecommunications prices follow the model of the
connect-hour charge in which the user pays an hourly rate
for the use of the online service over a telecommunication
network.

The price of printing and delivering database output offline to a user is expressed either as a flat rate
per record or per line printed.

Prices for features other than connect-time, telecommunications, and offline prints were introduced as the
sophistication of both the online services and their customer base increased. However, the price on which most
discount arrangements are based is still the price for the
use of the computer, plus overhead for related services
which make that use possible.

DISCOUNTS AND CONTRACTS OPTIONS AVAILABLE

Of the roughly five types of price discounts and
allowances (i.e., cash discounts, quantity discounts, functional discounts, seasonal discounts, and allowances),[1]
three apply to online information services: quantity discounts, seasonal discounts, and functional discounts.

Quantity discounts are offered to buyers who purchase in large volume. There are four types of quantity
discounts based on: (1) actual usage, (2) a commitment to
incur a certain level of connect-hour costs, (3) a subscription applied toward connect-hour costs, and (4) a
subscription to an indexing and abstracting service whose
database is available online.

A discount based on actual usage is calculated on
the number of searches conducted during prime time in one
month. The discount is a percentage reduction in the
total cost of prime time searches that escalates as the
number of searches increases. Some services previously
have offered a similar volume discount on connect-hour

price that escalated as the number of connect hours increased on one password in each month. Through quantity
discounts, services offer an incentive to the customer to
buy more from them rather than buying from multiple
sources. Discounts based on actual usage are not always
successful in obtaining customer loyalty.

To accomplish that, services offer discounts on the
price of computer time in exchange for a pledge to incur a
minimum amount of connect-hour costs over a fixed period
of time. These options are expressed in two ways: through
a commitment or pledge to incur a minimum amount of connect-hour costs, or through a prepaid subscription equal
to the amount of connect-hour costs that the customer
pledges to spend, at a minimum. The difference between
these options is best expressed in what the customer has
given to the service. In the commitment option, the customer has given the service a promise. In the subscription option, the customer has given the service money.

With some commitment options, the only risk the
customer takes is the loss of a discount for a given month
when connect-hour costs are below the threshold required
to receive the discount. Other commitment options involve
greater risk because the service invoices the customer at
the minimum level of connect-hour charges the customer
pledged to incur.

A subscription option requires prepayment of a sum
of money equal to the minimum level of connect-hour costs
the customer has pledged to incur over one year. The
online service may not be obligated to refund any unused
portion of the customer's subscription. Although exceptions are known to have been made, they are not guaranteed.

Most online services offer a subscription option.
Few online services offer a commitment option. Those that
offer a commitment option offer both options. One service
weighs the discount benefit heavily in favor of the subscription option, while another bases the discount in
favor of the commitment option. Both options involve risk
to the customer. Planning and research minimize those
risks. Selection of one of these options is generally
based on how much a service has been used in the recent
past, and on projections for how much of the service will
be used in the near future.

The discount benefits are significant and justify
the risk to a customer with sufficient usage. With few
exceptions, new customers should allow themselves sufficient time to use the service before making a commitment
or paying for a subscription.

The fourth type of quantity discount on connect-
hour price is based on a subscription to the printed products of an indexing and abstracting service. Some online
services are an outgrowth of an indexing and abstracting
service. In cases where the online service is sold directly by the indexing and abstracting organization, such as
Chemical Abstracts Service or H. W. Wilson, or in cases
where an indexing and abstracting company acquires databases produced by the Institute for Scientific Information
(ISI), study the price list for the online service to
determine where you may benefit.

All four types of quantity discounts reduce the
price of using the computer, whether that price is expressed in search charges or in cost per connect hour.
And the four options are not mutually exclusive. Contracts may reveal any combination of them. But most of
these methods require an active use of, and a sizeable
expenditure of funds on, the service.

Seasonal discounts are price reductions offered to
buyers who purchase merchandise or services out of sea-
son. Some online services discount the price of computer
time for "off-peak" use. This discount may be expressed
in either of two ways. A service either reduces the price
of the search charge or connect-hour price in off-peak
hours, or offers an alternative service that features a
reduced price for off-peak usage.

Services that employ a search charge offer a flat,
percentage-based reduction in the cost of a search during
off-peak hours. Other services reduce their connect-hour
price during off-peak hours on separate versions of their
service targeted for the enduser. The latter is not as
straightforward an option as the flat, percentage-based
discount. Look for versions of a traditional search service that the same company has developed for use by the
enduser. Although targeted for use outside of libraries
and information centers, these services are used by libraries for a host of reasons, not the least of which is
price reduction.

Enduser services may require a separate password
and documentation. They are excellent for the library
that wishes to introduce online services insofar as little
or no formal training is required, there is a minimum of
documentation, and costs are lower than those of the standard online service offered by the same company. They are
also widely used by the library that wishes to extend the
use of its online services directly to their own endusers

in the library. The one consideration to bear in mind is
that these are "off-peak" services, or, expressed in another way, they are not available during "peak" hours.

The definition of what constitutes an "off-peak"
hour will vary. Generally this refers to the evening and
early morning hours during the week, and to hours that the
service is made available during the weekend. It is very
important to establish how the definition of "off-peak"
service hours affects your library's ability to use the
service in your time zone.

The third type of price discount that applies to
online services is <u>functional discount</u>. Functional discounts are offered by a manufacturer to trade-channel
members in return for performance of certain functions
such as selling, storing, or recordkeeping. Library
networks that have organized a group contract for online
services receive a functional discount.

The discount that networks receive is a reduction
on the connect-hour price of online services. It is a
"functional" discount insofar as the network performs
urbain functions on behalf of the online service.
Usually, the network gathers sufficient prepayment from
its members to guarantee an annual subscription equal to
the connect-hour costs that the network pledges to incur.
The network deposits a subscription amount with the service on behalf of many separate online users. The network
pays the monthly invoice representing all of the costs
incurred by online users participating in the network's
group contract, minus a reduction on the connect-hour
price. The network then bills the user for all costs
incurred, less a portion of the discount on the connect-
hour price that the network has received from the service. Networks may promote the online service, or facilitate training for the online service, in the interest of increasing awareness of the benefits of online
services in general or of expanding the size of their
group contract for the service.

Functional discounts are offered by the service to
the library network. Each network uses its discretion to
determine price and contract options for libraries that
wish to benefit from their price reductions. Although the
search services may offer a list of library networks that
offer group contracts, specific information on price and
contract options are only available from the networks
themselves.

Our checklist of price discounts and allowances is
complete. As you shop for discounts keep the following in
mind:

1. The three types of discounts are mutually exclusive for each service. Quantity discounts apply to search charges or connect-hour costs, but not to the same charges in off-peak hours or to alternative services offered during off peak hours. You can benefit from the price reduction offered by a library network, but not on off-peak services. Quantity discounts originate from the online service; functional discounts are passed on through library networks.

2. The three types of discounts available appeal to different users:

    a) Quantity discounts are designed for medium to heavy users of a service.

    b) "Seasonal' or 'off-peak' discounts appeal to libraries that offer online services directly to the enduser, or that are interested in searching lower-priced versions of the main search system.

    c) Functional discounts appeal to light to medium users of a service who wish to benefit from the cost reduction offered by a group contract but do not use enough of a service to benefit from quantity discounts.

3. No service offers all types of discounts. The checklist highlights what is common among price reductions in many services.

4. Beware of hidden charges! Mailing charges, sign-up fees, monthly minimums, connect-hour and citation charges unbundled from database royalties—all need to be calculated as part of the overall cost of online searching. After all, you cannot save money searching on an apparent discount if you get hit with hidden, unanticipated charges.

5. Price discounts and allowances have changed for online services and will continue to evolve. Prices and price reductions today continue to reflect the use of an online service's mainframe computer. Recent developments in technology have enabled the customers of these services to rely upon high-speed modems, microcomputers, and CD-ROM to minimize their use of the service's mainframe computer, and to reduce the cost of online searching as a result. More sophisticated pricing methods such as "perceived value" are gaining recognition in the online industry, which reflects a greater maturity. If the pricing structure for online searching changes from a connect-time framework, contract options may change. For the present, however, this checklist will serve to guide the user through options currently available.

Note

1. Philip Kotler, Marketing Management: Analysis, Planning, and Control, 5th ed. (Englewood Cliffs: Prentice Hall, 1984), 515-522.

Do User Fees Affect
Searcher Behavior?

Brian Nielsen

A great change in attitude has occurred within the
past decade among reference planners and administrators
regarding the place of financial considerations in managing online search services. Ten years ago, it seemed to
many that the charging issue was an open question: maybe
we were going to find the means to offer online services
without charging. "Dollars and Sense," however, conveys a
decidedly pragmatic approach to online search administration, in which there is no question that dollars are involved. It seems to say that the fee or free issue should
be laid to rest, that a tougher, businesslike attitude is
more fashionable. I hope to help us see our situation in
relation to fees with a bit more openness, and with some
skepticism about the inevitability of that status quo
which has seemingly closed the fee or free debate for good.
Although my objective is in part to challenge the
passive acceptance of online search user fees, I have no
quibble with libraries' efforts to take a carefully measured approach in implementing pricing policies for online
and other expensive services. My library charges, just
like a great many other libraries, and at the time pricing
policies were implemented back in the early 1970s there
were really no other obvious policy options. This paper
is intended to challenge the field to think a bit more
deeply about the consequences of the policy choices in the
limited area of online search pricing as these choices
shape our larger public service program directions. In
the process it may appear that I am dusting off the old
chestnut of fee or free, but that is not at all the case.

What I write about is not whether it is good or bad to
charge a user for providing an online search; I rather
bring forward the question--What are the <u>concrete conse-
quences</u> of charging or not charging users for their
searches? Though the question of whether charging is good
or bad is effectively moot for most libraries, my question
is eminently relevant for today's manager who must assess
the actual effect of those policies on the library
services for which he or she is responsible.

This paper consists of three parts. First, I will
relate how the question of the consequences of fee-charging came to be formulated as I began exploring the topic
as a doctoral student some time back. Second, I will
present a theoretical perspective which places the question in a quite different light than that in which librarians are accustomed to viewing it. That theoretical
perspective is known as conflict sociology, and it challenges us to be far more objective in evaluating how we
provide service than we have been heretofore. Third, I
will describe briefly the research I undertook for my
dissertation, which showed significant differences in the
way librarians behaved, depending on whether they charged
for online searching. I will close my talk with a short
reflection on the implications of my research findings.

When I began asking this question--"What are the
actual consequences of charging or not charging user
fees?"--a few years ago as a student, I was quite sur-
prised at the dearth of hard research on it. The fee or
free issue had clearly generated intense heat at one time,
but very little light. How many studies were there which
attempted to carefully measure the significant changes
that occurred in user behavior when a library began charging for online searching? That I could find so few such
studies suggested two things to me: first, that the design
and implementation of such studies might be so complex as
to discourage many researchers from undertaking them, and
second, that it may be the case that the field didn't <u>want</u>
to know what the real consequences were of charging, as
knowing the answer might make new policy development that
much harder. By the late 1970s it appeared that the anti-
fee forces were losing, or rather, that the march of "prog-
ress" in the form of policy implementation to charge for
online had simply trampled them over. The value debate
became largely irrelevant as administrators felt pressure
to provide online searching but were not able to find
alternatives to fees to support the new service. In this
setting, what would be the point of finding out whether

fees have a negative impact? Put another way, it was
easier for library administrators (who play a major role
in setting the field's research agenda) to accommodate
differences if they were based on value grounds (belief
that charging for online is good or bad) than to accommodate differences in the face of real data supporting one
or the other position.

This train of thought really got me excited: Here
was an issue--fee or free--that an ALA president said was
so important that it struck to "the very foundation, not
only of our profession and services, but of individual
liberty," yet there was no significant research activity
on it. That no one else was working in this area not only
challenged me to proceed to design a research study, it
also led me to look specifically at the impact of a fee on
librarians' behavior. Since researchers in the field were
in a sense avoiding the obvious, policy relevant, and very
interesting question of what impact fees had, I felt that
looking at impacts of charging on librarians might
illuminate some deeper understandings about our field in
addition to providing some answers to the immediate research question. My research question thus came to be
formulated as: "Do librarians behave differently when they
are doing online searches for a fee than when they are
doing the same types of searches without charging for
them?"

It has been said that there is nothing quite so
practical as a good theory. To help sort out the relevant
variables from the many irrelevant ones, to suggest other-
wise unexpected relationships, and most of all to turn
data into meaning, theory is indeed essential. With a
strong interest in sociology and a hunch that other organizations and occupations faced related problems in charging for services, I looked into the sociology of work and
occupations as a source of theory. I did find what proved
to be an excellent framework for my research, conflict
sociology, and within that framework, a particular theory
relating to the behavior of professionals under the varying condition of whether clients pay them for services or
not. I would like briefly to describe that theory and the
broader framework in which it can best be understood.

Conflict sociology has emerged within the last
decade or so in sociology as a unifying framework for
understanding a wide variety of social phenomena. Its
central paradigm is what sociologists call stratification,
the idea that social relations of groups both large and

small can be described in terms of "higher" versus
"lower," "dominant" versus "submissive," or the jockeying
for position in terms of power or status. Conflict sociology directs researchers to look at such relationships
in analyzing social activity, as they a key to understanding the way such activity plays itself out. Marx was
a conflict sociologist of sorts, though contemporary conflict sociologists do not limit their scrutiny to only
economic stratification as Marx did, but look at a wide
variety of stratification relationships, such as those
exhibited by teachers versus students, government administrators versus citizen's groups, and businessmen versus
their customers.[1] An important stratification relationship for our purposes is that of professional versus
client.

For librarians to look at the professional-client
relationship as a conflict relationship has been virtually
unheard of, but I found it useful to look at it this way
in addressing the issue of the impact of fees on searcher
behavior. There are a great number of sociological and
public policy studies which base their hypotheses on the
existence of conflicting interests between professionals
and the groups they serve, and the news media have popular-
ized this viewpoint in regard to a number of professions,
such as certain types of medical specialties, lawyers, and
teachers. If all these "honorable" occupations have come
in for their licks, why should we see ourselves as particularly immune? Within the conflict sociology framework, the researcher Judith May has tried to formulate a
series of generalizations about how responsive professionals are to their clients, depending on whether the
clients pay for service themselves or the service is paid
for in some other way.[2]

May took examples from the medical profession
primarily. She showed how doctors who worked in private
practice, and thus earned their living through having
clients pay them directly for service, were more responsive to clients than physicians who worked in clinics
where there was no direct connection between the service
to the client and the salary the doctor earned. The doctor in private practice will listen to the explanation of
every ache and itch; he or she will be more solicitous in
attending to a nosebleed, a cold, or even an imagined
illness. Motivated at least in part by the realization
that the patient provides the fee, the private practi-
tioner may take to heart that famous dictum of the busi-

ness world, "The customer is always right." In contrast,
the clinic physician, paid either by an organization into
which all the clinic's clients pay, like an HMO, or by the
state in, say, a city hospital's emergency room, may not
be nearly so deferential, may in fact be abrupt in treat-
ing the patient's needs.

Note that within this theory there is not a value
judgement that being responsive is necessarily better; May
and others in medical sociology have remarked that too
much responsiveness runs counter to the notion of profes-
sionalism. The ideal of the professional is to make dis-
passionate decisions based on special and esoteric knowledge, not on the desires of the lay client. The professional is supposed to know better than the client what
is needed, and so to base responsiveness to the client's
desires on the nature of a financial transaction is to
undercut professional authority.

Limited time prevents me from elaborating further
on this theory; suffice it to say that I used the theory
to formulate a working hypothesis for my research, which
was as follows: Librarians who provide online search
service for a fee will be more responsive to their clients
than will librarians who provide online service without
charge to their user community. Let me now go on to describe how I went about collecting data to test this hypothesis.

I chose to conduct my research among selected U.S.
members of the Association of Research Libraries (ARL).
As a first stage in my study, I surveyed the 100 ARL-mem-
ber libraries to determine what fee structures were in
existence in the main reference departments of the libraries, and obtained information on such characteristics
as number of searches performed annually, size of the
general reference staff, and so on. Out of the 97 responses I received from this first survey, I found three libraries which could be defined as "free search" libraries,
where essentially no charges were levied for the great
majority of searches. Through a process of matching according to characteristics such as size of library, enrol-
lment size, and number of searches performed, I then chose
nine of what I called "fee libraries," libraries which
typically charged what it took to recover their search
costs, plus or minus some administrative fee or academic
discount. I excluded the provision of what we now commonly call "ready reference searches" from the categor-
izations made with these two groups of libraries. With

consent of all the librarians and administrators involved, I thus had 12 libraries employing over 85 librarians for the second stage of my study—three "free libraries" and nine "fee libraries."

My research hypothesis demanded that I determine some measure of librarian responsiveness. Using some common sense, the accepted wisdom in the online search literature, and values expressed frequently in the general literature of academic librarianship, I came up with six measures of activity which could be seen to be associated with responsiveness. These six measures were: 1) the amount of time the searcher spent with the user in the conduct of an online search (a positive association between time with user and responsiveness); 2) the amount of time the searcher spent overall on the online search (again a positive relationship); 3) the number of tasks performed in conjunction with the search, such as looking in a thesaurus, modifying a search, or notifying a user when his or her offline print came in (also a positive relationship); 4) the amount of continuing education activity the librarian engaged in (again positively related to responsiveness, as the self-renewing librarian is theoretically more responsive to user needs); 5) the amount of user education the librarian performs (positive again, as user education is presumably client-responsive); and 6) the amount of routine or clerical work the librarian performs, which would be associated negatively with client responsiveness, i.e., the more clerical work a reference librarian does, the less he or she is responsive to patron needs.

Having defined these six variables associated with responsiveness, I next undertook a survey of the 79 librarians who worked in general reference in the 12 libraries. I developed a questionnaire to find out how these librarians used their time, what they felt about charging for online searching, and how they were trained. I also created a form to enable these librarians to keep a sort of diary to record in detail what they did as they went about providing online searches, and asked that they fill in this form for the next five searches they did for users. With usable responses from 55 librarians, including diaries reflecting over 200 online searches, the 70% response rate was adequate to test my hypothesis.

What were this study's findings? While not all the measures of responsiveness resulted in conclusive evidence supporting the hypothesis, the study did find that in the libraries where fee-charging was established policy, the librarians were more responsive to their online search service clients, as measured by three of the responsiveness variables. This relationship was especially evident in the two variables measuring the amount of time the librarians took to conduct the searches--if the user pays, he or she gets more of the librarian's time, even if the noncharging libraries are offering what is at least thought to be the same type of online search service as the fee libraries. On the third responsiveness measure, the amount of continuing education the librarians engaged in, the fee-charging libraries also came out as more responsive by the definition the study established. These librarians attended more workshops, both online and other kinds, than the librarians in libraries which did not charge for online searches, thus we would expect them to be better trained to provide responsive service. All of these results were statistically significant at a .05 or better probability level.

Should these findings encourage library managers to maintain online service fees in order to have their reference librarians stay more responsive to their online users? In my view, absolutely not, since, as I noted earlier, "responsiveness" is not the only value that is important for good occupational practice. But that is not the only reason.

Aside from the greater amount of time the "fee" librarians spent with users on searches and the greater amount of continuing education they undertook, on other measures the fee-charging librarians were less responsive. The "no fee" librarians did more bibliographic instruction than the fee librarians, though the difference was not statistically significant. What was statistically, as well as conceptually, significant was that the librarians in the libraries which charged fees did more clerical work than the librarians in the libraries which offered online services without charge. This effect held even when clerical procedures involving the handling of money were discounted. Elsewhere I explore reasons why--based on a conflict sociological perspective--the fee-charging librarians do more clerical work than their free-service colleagues,[3] but this finding alone should make managers think twice about instituting charges, since they have long been concerned with reference librarians spending too much time on less-than-professional work.

What the study indicated overall was that although

librarians who work in situations where a fee is involved
are likely to be more responsive to fee-paying clients,
they are actually less responsive to the totality of
service demands in the workplace. The fee, in other words,
distorts the overall allocation of service provided in a
general reference department, as compared both to departments in which no fees are charged and to service ideals
as articulated in our literature.

It is difficult to say at this point how these
findings may inform new policy development in online
service delivery, if they are to have any impact at all.
The more widespread availability of enduser searching,
whether heavily subsidized by the institution or not,
clearly can significantly reduce the distortion caused by
online search fees. Similarly, the availability of set-
cost databases that are searchable without the use of
remote computing resources, such as those now becoming
available on optical disk, can enable librarians to allo-
cate their consulting services more equitably. A third
service design innovation which should be encouraged is
the use of appointment systems for non-fee services, such
as those we provide at Northwestern University through our
research consultation service.[4] Because we can expect
that the demand for information consulting services which
reference librarians are trained to provide will continue
to rise, it is especially important that we not lose sight
of the totality of information needs to which we are
especially well equipped to respond. We must take care to
weigh the allocation of service delivery based on our best
understanding of overall social value, rather than on the
monetary values which certain of our users are in a
preferred position to express. This, I think, will be a
great challenge for reference planners and library policy
administrators for the remainder of this century.

Notes

1. Randall Collins' Conflict Sociology: Toward an
Explanatory Science (New York: Academic Pr., 1975)
provides an excellent statement of this analytical
framework, and discusses a wide variety of research areas
to which the framework has been applied over the history
of sociology as a discipline.

2. Judith May, Professionals and Clients: A
Constitutional Struggle (Beverly Hills, Calif.: Sage,
1976).

3. The author's doctoral dissertation, "The Impact of a User Fee on Librarian Responsiveness: An Examination of Online Bibliographic Searching and Reference Practice," University of North Carolina, 1983, (UMI #83-16642) explores this finding at length. A book which reports this research in greater detail is expected to be completed in 1987.

4. These alternatives are elaborated on to some extent in Brian Nielsen, "Online Reference and 'The Great Change'." In Online Catalogs, Online Reference, Converging Trends: Proceedings of a 1983 LITA Preconference (Chicago: American Library Association, 1984), 74-88.

The Ripple Effect:
The Impact of Online
on Library Operations

Rebecca Kroll

I would like to take a more macroeconomic approach to online search, and discuss the impact of online on library services other than the online operation itself. When I first started work on this topic, I had in mind the picture of a rock thrown into a quiet pool creating ever-widening circles as the waves expand outward from the point of impact. While this is admittedly an inaccurate picture, since no one who has ever worked in a library could by any stretch of the imagination mistake it for a quiet pool, still the metaphor served as a starting point. Consequently, I was delighted when I came across reference to an article by William Pierce entitled "Effects of Technological Change: Exploring Successive Ripples," which I was sure would give me a useful introduction to this concept. Imagine my dismay when I began reading the article, in which Pierce introduces his subject with stimulating references to pig iron and blast furnaces. However, the article itself proved excellent. Pierce's contention is that "When innovations are adopted within existing systems of production, they may initiate pressures for successive 'ripples' of change in other parts of the system that offset or exaggerate the original impacts."[1] His theory applies equally well to engineering technology and to library technology.

Pierce goes on to discuss certain focal points in what he refers to as the "systems of production" where change is especially noticeable. He cites four major things to look for as a result of implemented technological change: 1) location of the activity, 2) efficiency of the activity, 3) conservation methods, and 4) bottle-

necks. In libraries, it is certainly true that location
changes: while ready reference searches may be done at the
reference desk, the bulk of online searching is conducted
away from the desk. In extreme cases a multi-branch library system may operate a centralized online service in
which all searches are done from the same office, replac-
ing manual searching done at dispersed units. We all
devoutly trust that efficiency has improved tremendously
as a result of online services. Conservation methods (including the storage and transfer of information) have
likewise changed. Pierce's final observation, that bottle-
necks appear in new and different locations, also holds
true for the library model: patrons now wait for a search
appointment or for offline prints where formerly they
waited for the latest paper index to arrive by mail. All
of these changes contribute to the ripple effect we are
discussing.

THE RIPPLE EFFECT

Online searching does not take place in a vacuum or
as an isolated activity. It may be shown on the library
organization chart as a separate entity reporting directly
to a head of public services, or as a section of the reference department; in either case, while a formal organization chart would show a link upwards along a single
reporting path, a less traditional "influence chart" might
show a web of dotted lines reaching out from online search
to reference, to interlibrary loan, to collection development, to facilities planning, and to library administration. All these areas are affected to some degree by
online search.

A logical starting point for an analysis of the
impact of online search is the reference desk itself. The
traditional reference query which began with a patron's
need for information, progressed through various stages of
question negotiation, recommendations of sources to use,
instruction in the use of those sources, and ended with
protracted manual searching of volumes, has been supplant-
ed by new forms of reference transactions. While not
every reference question does or should lead to an online
search, increasingly larger numbers of questions turn to
such searches as the most logical route to an answer.

Depending on the organizational structure of the reference department, the same librarian who first receives the query may follow it up as a search, or the patron may be referred to the search section of the department, or even to a separate department altogether. What formerly could have occupied hours of the patron's time, with repeated trips back to the reference desk for further instructions, may now be accomplished in a single session of less than an hour, even for a protracted bibliographic search.

For quick questions, the time may be closer to one minute than one hour, as more and more libraries turn to online for ready reference as well as bibliographic searching. We have evolved along a series of steps in the treatment of reference questions which can be expressed as a continuum, with the traditional one-on-one reference librarian/patron exploration of printed sources at one end. The first step towards online reference is usually the introduction of bibliographic database searching as a substitute for manual searching, using the online counterparts of the printed sources. A logical next step is the online search of numerical databases where the printout consists of the facts themselves rather than citations to the sources of the facts. From there we go to the online ready reference search performed at the reference desk on an ad hoc basis to gather quick facts, in preference to using the printed sources. Eileen Hitchingham did a survey in 1982 in which 25% of the libraries which responded had a terminal dedicated to ready reference.[2]

Another step in the overall progression is the introduction of the enduser search in which the patron performs the search after receiving instruction from the librarian, using the library's equipment. At the far end of the chain from the traditional reference transaction, completely outside the library, lies the "scholar workstation," where patrons in their own offices, using their own equipment, perform their own searches. Anathema to librarians? It shouldn't be.... The scholar workstation concept is simply one aspect of a series of possible ways to connect the patron and the information sought. To quote Klugman, "What emerges here is a picture of a continuum of information where no clear demarcation lines can be drawn between computer searching and traditional reference services and where there is a frequent spillover of one activity into the other."[3]

At the moment there are libraries operating at all points on the continuum, some remaining relatively static, some progressing rapidly and enthusiastically towards the

far end. For those somewhere in the middle using varying
degrees of online search with the librarian as intermediary between the patron and the data, there are many
factors to consider in analyzing the impact on the reference department. Spillover within the reference department can affect both the reference patron and the reference staff. One possible effect upon staff, depending
on how the online operation is set up, is the potential
for a division between searchers and nonsearchers in a
department where not all of the librarians work online.
Like the bibliographer/nonbibliographer schism which has
occurred in some libraries where collection development
responsibilities have been bestowed on some librarians
while others do purely reference, a caste system may also
develop which distinguishes staff with online expertise
from those without online experience.

Even when the entire department enthusiastically
embraces the online experience, there are still adjustments to be made in the day-to-day routine: it takes
longer to prepare for and run an online search of <u>Psychological Abstracts</u> than it does to show a patron how to use
the paper index. This shift from impromptu instruction in
the use of sources as part of reference desk duty to preplanned searching away from the desk necessitates a change
in overall use of staff time. The administration of the
online operation is in itself a time-consuming but critically important part of the operation, since costs must
be scrutinized and quality monitored on an ongoing basis
to insure a successful operation. Gone are the days when
a hard-copy subscription was paid once a year, then forgotten until the next year's invoice arrived. From the
administrative point of view, online operations require
constant attention lest they get completely out of hand.

Patrons, also, feel the effects of the change. In
most cases the change has been a happy one, with better
results obtained from much less time spent, and for the
most part at a cost which is not a burden. For some library users, however, the costs of an online search may be
a genuine barrier. Another negative point for some patrons is that unless they are in a library where enduser
search is already the norm, online introduces a barrier in
the form of a librarian who comes between them and the
database, so that they are one step removed from the research process. Many patrons find it frustrating that all
of their modifications to the process must seemingly be
approved by the librarian who translates them into
acceptable language for the search. The final blow, from

the patron's point of view, falls when the fabulous system
which has been touted as guaranteed to give stupendous
results is "down" just at the moment of greatest need.
Any librarian working with either online searching or an
automated catalog will know the feeling of frustration
when one reaches for the wonders of modern technology only
to discover that the aforementioned wonders have decided
to take a prolonged holiday. Repairing a broken binding
on a volume of <u>Statistical Reference Index</u> is child's play
compared to trying to predict when the storm over the West
Coast will ease off and allow telecommunications to be
resumed.

Reference collection management is also not exempt
from the impact of online services. In this day of less-
than-ideal budgets, most libraries have looked hungrily at
reference serial subscriptions with a view to allowing
them to be replaced by online access. The selection process for reference tools has become more complex, because
in addition to asking whether or not our patrons would use
any given item, we must also ask ourselves in which format
it should be made available. As a hard copy index? As an
online database only? As an online database backed up by
a paper copy? On disc for direct access by patrons?
There are two kinds of decisions involved here... 1) whether or not to renew a subscription, and in what format(s),
and 2) whether to begin a subscription to a promising new
service (and if so, it goes almost without saying, what to
cancel to make room for it in the budget)? After survey-
ing a sampling of university, research, and special libraries, Lancaster determined that "the availability of
online access has so far had a rather minor effect in
causing libraries to cancel subscriptions to print on
paper."[4] In Hitchingham's survey, on the other hand,
40% of the responding libraries reported cancelling subscriptions because of online search capabilities.

Technology has further complicated our lives with
the advent of optical disc storage of data. The CD-ROM
and 12-inch discs which now cover newspapers, general
interest periodicals, and business journals, to name but a
few, make it easy for the patron to search unassisted by a
librarian. Some offer a choice of either a menu-driven
approach which guides the user easily through each step of
the search or a standard search option using protocols
designed for the experienced user. The benefits of the
optical disc approach are numerous, but their very existence adds another twist to the decision process for reference collection management. Because the subscription

costs are still so high, careful consideration must be
given to the projected uses for the system, especially in
an industry where there are two formats. At least the
music industry has standardized its output!

Given that the library has somehow miraculously
settled on a choice or a blend of online search and optical disc access, the ripples are still expanding as we
enter the realm of the general collection. Does the library have the materials, especially the more esoteric
journals, to back up the computerized bibliographic
sources now available? Having just affirmed that both
online search and discs have high associated costs, we are
now about to incur more expenses by trying to make available to the patron all the wonderful articles he or she or
we have found. Since the days of the infinitely elasti-
cized budget are over, this usually leads us to the door
of the interlibrary loan office, which then needs to be
propped open using more staff! While opinion is mixed as
to whether ILL volume is or is not increased by online
searching, ILL staffing is nevertheless a facet to consider when reconstructing the ripple effect. One factor
which tends to limit the impact of online searching on ILL
is that the CONTU (Commission on New Technological Uses of
Copyrighted Works) Guidelines to the Copyright Law pro-
hibit using ILL for more than limited numbers of recent
articles from any given title. Thus online searching,
with its emphasis on current material, may create a demand
which is difficult to satisfy internally and illegal to
satisfy using external sources, other than by referring
the patron in person to another library.

A discussion which lists only the departments
adjacent to online services would be overlooking online's
repercussions on the library administrative process. As
Lewis observes in an article on management of online resources, "Online systems...are not just what we have now,
only more so."[5] In order for online to be managed, not
just adequately, but effectively, library administrators
need clearer goals than simply, "We want to go online--how
do we get there?" Integrating online services smoothly
and successfully into the full scheme of library services
is an excellent example of change management, because it
embodies so many aspects of change: a different method of
doing library work, probably a different place for doing
it, possibly even different people joining the organization because of it. Add to this the fact that online
itself is constantly developing, which means that librarians must also constantly grow, develop new skills, and

learn new techniques and new systems. New databases spring
up seemingly overnight, established but little-used ones
quietly vanish, and flourishing ones are reloaded in improved formats at the will of the publishers.

All of this simply illustrates what we know only
too well, which is that managing online service is not a
one-time, set-it-and-forget-it operation. And as our use
of online reference changes, so our philosophy of library
service evolves. As we move from one end of the reference
continuum to the other, we move away from the reference
librarian as the source of all knowledge, the intermediary
through whom researchers must work, towards the reference
librarian as facilitator and educator, helping patrons
learn how to help themselves. Instead of seeing scholar
workstations and enduser systems as threats to our profession, we can and should take a leadership role on our
campuses, in our districts, and in our companies in promot-
ing new modes of research and information access.

FUNDING

All of this is very well in theory, but we are still
faced with the eternal question: Where does the money come
from? Now we come to the financial ripples caused by online: the need for adequate funding in times of shrinking
budgets, leading to the philosophical issue of charging for
online service, and to an examination of possible funding
alternatives.

Any discussion of funding should start with the big
picture--the economic environment of the library in which
the online service operates. Drake and Olsen break down
the economic environment into external factors, institutional setting, and factors internal to the library.[6]
External factors include the overall economic climate,
whether growth or recession, political attitudes and government funding, the current state of population growth,
and recent technological developments.

The institutional setting consists of the company,
district, or campus where the library operates, and where
it frequently meets with increasing competition for funds.
Academic libraries are sensitive to this issue because
there is conflict among research, teaching, and support
activities on any campus as to how institutional funds
should be shared; the tendency is for research activities

to win out because they, in turn, bring in more funding
from outside. Public libraries have to compete with fire
protection and law enforcement for their share. School
libraries all too often come off a poor second to athle-
tics. Libraries in a corporate setting may operate on the
basis of charging all direct and indirect costs back to
the department which uses the service, in which case their
major battle is for funds to establish or upgrade the online service rather than for ongoing support.

Internal factors include the library's total operating budget, the political clout of online within the
library, and the growing need to "find" funds inside the
library through increased efficiency rather than to request more and more budget increases.

In a 1983 paper, Evans cites ongoing operational
costs of online ranging from $8,800 (public library) to
$28,000 (corporate library) annually.[7] He reviews ar-
ticles on funding methods, which fall along a line ranging
from total subsidy by the library at one end to total cost
recovery at the other end. He also distinguishes between
start-up costs and ongoing costs; given adequate advance
planning, start-up costs can sometimes be handled with a
grant (possibly tied to networking) to help pay for equipment, or with a one-time allocation from the parent institution built into the regular annual budget. Evans
notes that cancellation of printed indexes may free up
funds for ongoing expenses, with the caveat that in some
libraries monies in the collection budget cannot be trans-
ferred to other areas. He also notes that in an effort to
circumvent such cancellations, some database producers
"impose a multi-tiered price structure based on continuing
subscriptions to the printed indexes," and cautions that
"cancellations alone will be insufficient to subsidize all
searching."[8]

We are left accordingly with the library still
somewhere along the cost-recovery line. Looking internally first, the more the library wants to subsidize online services, the more necessary it is to find funds in
the regular library budget. Even if the library administration is fully committed to completely subsidized
searching, the department in charge of online must still
fight the myth that computerization makes it acceptable to
cut staff. In one survey, over 75% of library managers
agreed that online service increases staff productivity,[9]
This is true up to a point, especially if the librarian
were to do the manual searching in any case, but it does
not necessarily hold true if online search is an alter-

native to patrons doing their own manual searching. As Cogswell notes, "A typical online search requires close to one hour of staff time, of which only fifteen minutes on average is spent in performing the actual computer search."[10] It is the indirect and frequently undocumented costs associated with staff time which make budgeting for online complex.

Given that the library has identified some or most of the costs of online, and has exhausted its internal resources, the next move may be to pass all or some of the charges on to the patrons. Immediately two sources of controversy spring up. Should library users be expected to bear the cost of online search in any way? If so, should costs be borne solely by those who personally use the service, or should the overall costs be spread out among all users who may potentially benefit from the existence of the service, in the form of higher overdue fines or service fees?

The philosophical battle of "to charge or not to charge" has been raging almost from the moment online search became available to users. One compelling argument in favor of charging is that it may be the only way the library can afford to provide online services at all. Another justification is that patrons are paying for the speed and efficiency of the service, not for the information itself, which could have been obtained by other methods. Online charges are seen as equitable in that those who benefit more pay more than those who use the service little or not at all. Many libraries pass on interlibrary loan charges to their patrons; passing on online charges is seen as falling into the same category.

On the other side the arguments are equally varied One argument against charging is the philosophical view of information as a "public good" which should be available at all times. In his book Management Control in Nonprofit Organizations, Robert Anthony draws a parallel between the supply of information and the light supplied by a lighthouse: while there are certain costs attached to maintaining each, both are "public goods" in the sense that they are there to benefit all of society, and no matter how many people benefit, the supply is never used up. The lighthouse continues to produce its warning whether no ship approaches or a dozen freighters navigate by its light; the supply of information is there whether no one opens a book or the library is busy at all hours.[11]

A similar philosophy was expressed by the National Commission for Libraries and Information Science in 1978:

as an ideal, the National Program would strive to
eventually provide every individual in the United
States with equal opportunity of access to that
part of the total information resources which will
satisfy the individual's educational, working,
cultural and leisure-time needs and interests,
regardless of the individual's location, social or
physical condition, or level of intellectual
achievement.[12]

Using this statement many librarians argue that charging
for online may promote efficiency but not equity, since it
places a disproportionate burden on low-income patrons who
may have the most need of the library's help but are the
least able to pay for that help.

Another interesting argument is that charging for
services actually increases the library's costs, first
because the administration of a fee-based service is in
itself time-consuming and costly. Secondly, as Cooper and
DeWath discovered, there is some evidence that overall
costs to the library increase when search fees are charged
because staff spend more preparation time for even less
online time than they do for free searches, feeling that
patrons' expectations are raised by the imposition of
charges.[13]

Online costs consist of variable and fixed costs.
Fixed costs are those which remain constant regardless of
the number of searches done, such as equipment leases,
charges for modems and telephone lines dedicated to online, and salaries of staff assigned full-time to online
services. Variable costs are those which change as the
volume of searching changes: online charges for actual
time linked to the database, citation charges, paper supplies used in printing, and staff time used for searching
if this time has to be taken away from other activities.
While some libraries may be able to handle one-time start-
up costs and even absorb fixed costs into the regular budget, the variable costs are more difficult to absorb since
they are at the same time unpredictable and very conspicu-
ous. Frequently libraries which "charge for online service" are actually only passing on these variable costs to
the patron.

Without trying to resolve here the conflicts over
online charges, let us pass on to the outermost level of
the library's economic environment—the outside world. In
Funding Alternatives for Libraries,[14] Breivik and Gib-

son have collected essays discussing outside sources of
funding, including funds from Friends of the Library organizations, endowments, gifts, telethons, foundation grants,
and corporate gifts. The corporate approach is particularly tempting just now, with corporate giving reaching
new heights: the American Association of Fund-Raising
Counsel Annual Report for 1984 shows total philanthropy
occurring on the scale of $74 billion dollars for 1984, as
opposed to the 1974 total of $26 billion--almost a three-
fold increase; $10 billion of the 1984 total went to ed-
ucation, which should make academic libraries in particular
take notice.

Nitecki notes that in addition to looking for gifts,
online services can aim at becoming self-supporting by
offering fee-based information services either to individuals outside the usual clientele or to companies in the
private sector.[15] This last approach, of course, is not
recommended for special libraries unless their own company
happens to be in the information industry!

This leads to the point that while virtually all
libraries with online services need funding for their
operations, not all libraries function alike or can operate under the same guidelines. The public, the academic,
and the corporate library have different priorities to
meet. To the special library, speed and accuracy of
information, possibly combined with confidentiality, may
outweigh all considerations of cost, since increases in
online costs can ultimately be passed to the consumer
through product pricing. The academic library tries to
support the demands of research and teaching, both pressed
for funds, and in varying degrees of haste. The public
library has the broadest range of all, since it is called
upon to help local companies, local students, private
researchers, freelance writers, and others, all doing
legitimate research, as well as meeting the needs of
recreational readers.

Corporate libraries can protect their online turf
through cost justification and proofs of efficiency.
Academic libraries can draw on alumni resources and ma-
neuver for a piece of the institutional pie, as well as
look to direct grants for online services. While outside
funding from grants may also be available to public libraries, for the most part they are faced with creating
enough support among users for online services that these
same users will help them in their fight for funding.

CONCLUSION

Whether a given library finds itself consistently scrambling for funds just to keep the online operation going, or consistently getting grants, finding seed money, and leading the way in enhancements to the use of new technology, may reflect not just an abundance or absence of funds, but the library's prevailing internal philosophy towards the place of online in the library and the role of the library in society.

In conclusion, the impact of online goes well beyond library economics alone. It impinges on staff morale, enhances our degree of professional pride, alters the definition of the library, and expands the influence of the library on its environment. Online can be the vehicle which propels the librarian from the role of intermediary and interpreter into the role of leader-teacher-innovator. As one dean of a graduate school recently expressed it, "The library should develop a strong proprietary/cooperative role toward new information systems as these systems emerge. If it is a medium that has to do with knowledge . . . the library ought to be there ready and waiting to take it over."[16] The most positive ripple effect I can imagine from online services is the transformation of the library from a reactive position as a passive storehouse of knowledge into an active role as a leader in information technology development.

Notes

1. William S. Pierce, "Effects of Technological Change: Exploring Successive Ripples." In Bela Gold, ed., Technological Change: Economics, Management and Environment (New York: Pergamon Press, 1975), 149-168.

2. Eileen Hitchingham et al., "A Survey of Database Use at the Reference Desk," Online 8(2):44 (March 1984).

3. Simone Klugman, "Online Information Retrieval Interface with Traditional Reference Service," Online Review 4(3):267 (September, 1980).

4. F. W. Lancaster and Herbert Goldhor, "The Impact of Online Services on Subscriptions to Printed Publications," Online Review 5(4):310 (August, 1981).

5. D. A. Lewis and R. Adkins, "The Management of Online Resources: Problems and Opportunities," Online Review 5(5):370 (October, 1981).

6. Miriam A. Drake and Harold A. Olsen, "Economics of Library Innovation," Library Trends, special issue on The Economics of Academic Libraries (Summer 1979): 93.

7. John E. Evans, "Methods of Funding." In James J. Maloney, ed., Online Searching: Technique and Management (Chicago: ALA, 1983), 143.

8. Ibid., 141.

9. Rebecca Whitaker, "The Impact of Online Search Services in Libraries." In Maloney, op. cit., 169.

10. James A. Cogswell, "Online Search Services: Implications for Libraries and Library Users," College & Research Libraries 39(4):276 (July 1978).

11. Robert Newton Anthony, Management Control in Nonprofit Organizations, (Homewood, Ill:, R. D. Irwin, 1984), 184.

12. National Commission on Libraries and Information Science, Toward a Program for Library and Information Services: Goals for Action, an Overview (Washington: 1978).

13. Michael D. Cooper and Nancy A. DeWath, "Effect of User Fees on the Cost of Online Searching in Libraries," Journal of Academic Librarianship 10(4):304 (December 1977).

14. Patricia Senn Breivik and E. Durr Gibson, eds., Funding Alternatives for Libraries (Chicago: ALA, 1979).

15. Danuta A. Nitecki, "Academic Libraries, Online Searching, and Turf: A Symposium," Journal of Academic Librarianship 11(5):274 (November 1985).

16. Clyde Hendrick, "The University Library in the Twenty-first Century," College & Research Libraries 47(2):130 (March 1986).

Simultaneous Remote Searching: The Oregon Connection—Skilled Intermediary Delivery of Online Services in a Multitype Library Network

Verl A. Anderson and Deborah L. Graham

THE ISSUE

For several years now, major news magazines have informed the American public and American libraries of the ease of access and usefulness of online computer services. However, the growth of these services has been slowing.

Why then haven't these online or dial-up electronic computer services enjoyed the rapid expansion in use that has been repeatedly predicted? Librarians in the field who routinely work with these systems know one answer. Whether the dial-up service is an electronic mail system, a bibliographic search service, or a "hard-data" computer source, actual use of the system presents predictable common problems:

1. All dial-up systems are not the same. Even when subscribing to a major "vendor" service, there will often be differences in the actual command names, and in how commands function from one database on a system to another. Very few individuals, even trained online experts, can function with ease and cost-effective precision on multiple systems. And since "time is money" on dial-up systems, hesitation or confusion can be very expensive.

2. Telecommunications skills are not widely available. Most potential public users of dial-up systems will need some assistance just in learning how to set up their equipment and use the national networks. Most dial-up service vendors, long accustomed to working with trained personnel, do not realize the depth of a novice's

confusion in making the first online call, and have not
provided sufficient information to help effectively.
Should an individual still have difficulties, it is often
hard to reach anyone who can do effective "trouble-shooting." In small rural communities, even the vendor may be
new to dial-up computer communications. Sacred Heart
General Hospital Library has been called on to trouble-
shoot unfamiliar equipment in three rural communities, and
successfully advised vendors on the need for stronger car-
rier tone signals and checking for faulty cables.

   3. All individuals who access systems do not do so
with the same degree of expertise. Expertise is generally
related to frequency of access and skill in requiring the
system to perform at its full potential. The present
industry solution to the problem of "unskilled" users has
been the development of user-friendly frontends. While
these enable novices to access systems, we have found in
all cases to date that the frontend limits the actual
usefulness and accuracy of the database, acting inadver-
tently as a form of "governor" or unintentional censor.

   In brief, while the publicity would suggest that
dial-up computer services are relatively inexpensive and
easy to use, this is not the case in actual practice.

THE OREGON SOLUTION

   Through Simultaneous Remote Search (SRS), origi-
nated at Sacred Heart General Hospital Library in 1982,
and implemented at Eastern Oregon State College (EOSC) in
1983, Oregon has expanded the availability of online computer search services. Simultaneous Remote Search (SRS),
utilizes a Trialog switch. The Trialog switch allows a
trained searcher at one location to log in to national
database systems, and, at the same time, transmit all
interactions to a third "requestor" site in another part
of the state. Untrained primary users can receive the
online print, and watch and even comment on the search as
it progresses.

   SRS services are now being further expanded through
an LSCA grant administered by EOSC to include 28 academic,
public, and health service libraries in the eastern 10-
county region of Oregon. The area served occupies 42,000
square miles (46% of the state's land mass) and is equivalent in size to the State of Kentucky. It is a rural area

of great geographic diversity with widely scattered communities and includes only 6% of the state's population.

By using sound business principles of distributive
processing and specialization for optimal use of personnel, the Oregon solution has put high touch back into high
tech and made online search services available to sites
without onsite trainer personnel.

In addition to "real-time" Simultaneous Remote
Searching, the trained searchers can forward search results via electronic mail. Potential online "customers"
get exactly what they want through their own computer
terminals without knowing a single online command. In
short, the librarians become the user-friendly, cost-
effective intermediaries for search requestors.

SPECIFIC TECHNIQUES OR EXAMPLES

1. Simultaneous Remote Searching
    A not untypical request, which illustrates both
    the function of SRS and its practicality, was
    recently made by Wallowa Memorial Hospital....
    The hospital called and said that a doctor was
    on his way to the hospital to deliver twins,
    but had never before performed other than
    single deliveries. The doctor requested
    information via telephone from his office
    before leaving for the hospital in regard to
    specific problems he might anticipate with the
    delivery.... By the time he arrived at the
    hospital 15 minutes later, there were 26
    article citations with abstracts waiting for
    him. The twins, both boys, arrived safely.[1]
2. Interactive Simultaneous Remote Searching (ISRS)
    A hospital librarian needing a search on a
    business database that she uses very
    infrequently calls an "expert" searcher at
    Eastern Oregon State College. With that
    connection made, the hospital librarian can log
    in on her own BRS ID code, and then turn over
    the running of the search to the remote
    expert. ISRS allows the "pooling" of subject
    and database expertise, resulting in better and
    less expensive search results all around.
        A new liaison library manager in a small

Oregon town is just learning to use the electronic mail system. She has tried several times, unsuccessfully, to transmit a message to the Sacred Heart search center in Eugene, Oregon. She calls the Eugene search center for help. The center connects her terminal to theirs, logs in to the electronic mail system, and turns the keyboard over to the remote trainee. After watching her procedure for sending a message, the center sees that she is not using the correct commands. By trouble-shooting trainee problems when they happen, the ISRS technique improves the relevance and impact of online training.

3.   Store and Forward

Early one morning, a physician in an outlying community sends a message to the search center in Eugene, requesting articles on physical examinations for high school athletes. The search center picks the message up along with other routine mail at 10 a.m. By 4 p.m. that afternoon, the completed online search--a list of 20 citations--is loaded into the physician's mailbox, ready for him to pick up that evening. The next day, the center receives a message asking for copies of items "1, 7, and 13." Those articles are mailed out the same day.

POTENTIAL APPLICATIONS IN OTHER SETTINGS

Specific advantages of the intermediary assisted systems described are:

1.   The best and most cost-effective use of existing resources, especially of trained manpower.
2.   Immediate consumer gratification that still allows for individually paced and directed growth.
3.   More rapid exposure of the public to systems that presently require more training and practice than most individuals are willing to commit.

Systems such as that being used in Oregon are easily replicated in other areas, and in a variety of library types. The technique of providing on-site, real-time online search access, and of using the requestor's ID codes while providing expert manpower, may greatly expand the role of public library online searchers, but avoid the controversy of "connect-time" charging. By acquainting the public gradually with dial-up access, and providing human assistance during the learning stage, the development of public online literacy can be accelerated. The use of intermediaries in online systems can in fact function in much the same way as the telephone operator did in the early development of the telephone. Intermediaries can constitute a new form of "Hello Central," where online needs can be referred and addressed with minimal user stress. As users gain in online literacy, intermediaries can assist in the development of systems that are not based on traditional printed information patterns, and have great potential to reduce float time in critical scientific fields.

Note

1. Verl A. Anderson, "Simultaneous Remote Searching," Library Journal 110(18): 167-169 (November 1, 1985).

Bibliography

Harris, Catherine. "Information Power: How Companies are Using New Technologies to Gain a Competitive Edge." Business Week (Oct. 14, 1985): 108-114.

Kiechel, Walter III. "Everything You Always Wanted To Know May Soon Be On-Line." Fortune (May 5, 1980): 226-240.

Trautman, Rodes, and Christie King. "Interactive Simultaneous Remote Searching: Evolution of Conference Call Searching to a Reliable Procedure." Online (September 1983): 90-97.

_____, and Deborah L. Graham. "Three-Party Telecommunications to Facilitate Public Use of Interactive Systems." ASIS Proceedings, Las Vegas, Nevada, October 1985: 258-261.

Toward Better Online Reference Statistics:
Getting Computers to Do the Work

Elizabeth A. Titus

What's the average cost of a search? How many
searches have been done this fiscal year? Can you tell me
which departments on campus are doing searches? How many
of the searches are charged to departmental accounts and
how many are direct payments? Which databases are searched
most frequently? Which vendors do we actually use?

These are typical questions frequently asked by library managers who need "statistical" information to make
programmatic decisions on library online reference services.

However, the gathering and reporting of online
reference statistics which provide meaningful information
on answering these questions is indeed managerially challenging! Some of the pragmatic constraints that online
reference service providers face in obtaining usable statistics include:

Limited experimental base. Online reference
services have not been around that long. We still
are defining and identifying what it is we really
need to measure.

Lack of standardization of terms. On an online
services survey or questionnaire, you are
frequently asked what appears to be a simple
question: How many searches do you do? However,
the question that isn't asked and should be is,
"What do you count as a search?" Libraries,
unfortunately, vary widely in what they count as a
search. Some are counting every file or every

session number as a search. More frequently a
search is considered to be a patron user contact in
which one search can result in looking at more than
one file.

Both Northern Illinois University (NIU) and Oakland
University count only patron user contacts that
result in an actual search in compiling fee-for-
service online reference services statistics. If a
patron set up an appointment for a search and for
some reason did not get a search done, that patron
contact is recorded at the reference desk as a
reference question. Always write down and define
your terms. Make sure everyone who is involved in
the statistical gathering process understands what
is being counted.

Increasing levels of complexity. Many of our online reference services started out modestly, with
online searches available from one or two primary
vendors. However, we have grown rapidly and now
provide much more sophisticated online reference
services to our users. Increasingly, we are using
more vendors, providing ready reference services,
and providing end-user search services as well.
This results in an increased need by library managers for more detailed statistical information on
these service areas.

Limited staff support. In many libraries, online
reference services were initiated on "shoestring"
operational budgets or were considered to be
add-ons to General Reference Department services.
From an administrative perspective, it is frequently the case that online reference service
operations which are "paperwork" intensive have
minimal or inadequate levels of clerical staff
support. You frequently hear from online reference
managers that it would be nice to have more detailed statistics on our services, but we just do
not have the staff to do it. We are too busy providing the services, keeping our search analysts
updated and trained, and keeping our search manuals
updated!

In fall 1985, Northern Illinois University Libraries
began using a computerized statistical maintenance system

(CSMS) for its Computer Reference Service. The CSMS,
which has been in development since 1979 at Oakland University Libraries, Rochester, Michigan, uses a computerized statistical package (SPSS:Statistical Package for the
Social Sciences and PFS:GRAPH which reduces the amount of
personnel time required to gather and process data, stream-
lines statistical reporting structure, and provides more
information critical to making more informed management
decisions.

The CSMS was initially designed with some basic
premises in mind, which included:

> Consider any library statistic you keep to be part
> of a system—a library management system. If you
> keep any piece of statistical information, it
> should provide you with meaningful information that
> is used to make management decisions.

> Use available technology. Computers can manipulate,
> store and do mathematical functions more efficiently
> than humans. Use computers as much as possible to
> keep your library statistics.

> Integrate the ongoing tasks associated with gather-
> statistical information into the daily work process
> as much as you can.

> Gather the information on an ongoing basis, but
> only ask for reports when you really need to do so.

> The CSMS, although initially intended for Oakland's
> needs, should be easily adaptable to meet other
> libraries' statistical maintenance needs.

> The system should be easy to maintain—so easy a
> student could do it.

There were basically three phases of development
for the design of this statistical maintenance system:
planning and design, implementation, and review and
analysis.

Phase 1. Planning and Design

One of the first tasks was to determine what data needed to be kept and what we wanted the reports to look like. These answers permited us to design the code configurations and data input and output formats for creating our SPSS program.

By looking at Table 1, you can get a basic idea of what data NIU Libraries Computer Reference Search Services wanted to collect. A decision was made to use the same definitions for each of the variables fields that Oakland University's library was using so that institutional comparisons could be made.

Table 1   NIU Libraries/Computer Reference Services
Code Configurations List as of 9/11/85

Column	Variable Label
1-2	Searcher Code
3-4	Year
5-6	Month
7-8	Day
9-11	Sequential # for transaction
12-14	Time (in minutes) for interview
15-17	Time (in minutes) for information
18-20	Time (in minutes) for post-search activities
21	Systems Used
22-23	# Files Search
24-26	Time online (rounded up in minutes)
27-29	# online citations
30-32	# pages printed offline
33	SDI
34-38	Total Cost of Search
39-41	Campus Office/Department Code
42	Method of Payment
43-52	Account Number
53-54	Type of User
55-56	Purpose of Search
57-58	Subject Area

Phase 2. Implementation

Rather than do our own programming and risk becoming too "programmer dependent," we chose to use a well established statistical package that was reputable and likely to be available on most academic campuses. SPSS fit the bill. At Oakland, the necessary SPSS programming was done by the systems librarian. AT NIU, the programming was done by a graduate assistant. These same individuals were also responsible for doing data processing. Students were trained to do the data input.

During this second phase, the "mechanics" of how data were to be gathered were addressed. The patron, the search analyst, and the computer reference services coordinator and/or staff all contribute in some way to the data gathering process.

Also key to this process was the design of the Computer Reference Request Form illustrated in Table 2. All information that eventually will be coded is located somewhere on this form.

Some basic lessons were learned as we used this method for gathering our data over several years. Searchers are advised to always check that the person they are doing the search for has completely filled out the search request form. Also, search analysts should not wait too long after they have done a search to catch up on the paperwork associated with that search. It gets more difficult with time to reconstruct information about what you did on a specific search.

It is best to do coding and data imputting in small segments on a systematic basis. The objective is not to have a lot of processing work at the end of the statistical year.

Phase 3. Review and Analysis

This is perhaps the most exciting part of the process --you not only see what the statistical run produces, but you work with graphics software to "package" your product.

Remember that the data has been gathered and input on a continuous basis throughout the entire statistical reporting year, which in this case is July 1 through June

Table 2   NIU Libraries/Computer Reference Services
            Search Request Form Categories

Done at the time the online search request form is filled
out by the patron:

> Name/Address/Phone
> Method of Payment/Account No.
> Type of User
> Purpose of Search

Done at various stages of the search process by the
individual search analyst:

> Search Code
> Year/Month/Day
> Transaction #
> Interview, Formulation,
> Post-Search Time
> Systems Used
> SDI
> Cost of Search

Done after search has been completed
by the online reference service staff:

> Does Coding
> Inputs Data
> Does Program Run

---

30. However, the program which does all the counting,
tabulation, and report generation is run only on a need
basis, as Table 3 illustrates. Usually, the program is
run at the end of the fall term, the end of the winter
term, and after June 30. We have reduced the amount of
paperwork, staff time, filing, etc., just by reducing the
frequency of reporting.
     Although the SPSS printouts are circulated intern-
ally to those who are interested in reviewing them, the
printout is considered to be an internal working document.
     Let's look at some examples of the online refer-
ence services CSMS reports that are generated and the

Table 3   NIU Libraries CRS Statistical Reporting Scheme
           Comparison of Past and Current Practices

Prior Reporting Scheme

    Computer Reference Service
    12 times a year monthly report sent to:
        Department
        Division
        Library Administration
    routed to:
        Searchers Group

Once a year annual report sent to all above

Current Reporting Scheme

    Computer Reference Service does SPSS run
    approximately three times a year

    Annual run only kept on file in unit and
    in administration files.

---

graphs done from these reports. The SPSS reports reflect
one year of activity. However, as these reports are generated in successive years, the graphs can easily be updated to show activity over a timeline.
        A variety of reports can be generated using SPSS
which permit you to look at your data from different
perspectives and at varied levels of detail. Typically,
most online services units want to look at their monthly
search activity. With one of the SPSS report options you
can obtain absolute frequencies by month (Fig. 1). On
this type of report you also get relative frequencies,
adjusted frequencies, and cumulative frequencies, as well
as other statistical information such as the mean, the
mode, the median, and the standard deviation.
        Once you have your data from the SPSS reports, it
is suggested that you take this "raw data" and convert it
into "presentation-quality" graphics. If you have a micro-

computer, there are several good graphics software packages now on the market that are easy to use and affordable.

Whether you have a microcomputer or not, you should try to use graphics when presenting statistical data if at all possible. Too frequently, an enormous amount of time is spent tabulating data, but not enough time is spent on presenting information so that it is understandable.

At NIU we use two graphics packages, PFS:Graph and Graphics Department to generate area, line, scatter, xy, pie, or bar charts. Both software packages are easy to learn and will permit you to do fairly sophisticated graphics.

Using Graphics Department "whenever you plot a scatter, line, area, or bar chart, you have an opportunity to plot some additional statistics on the chart. These optional statistics [Fig 2.] include the mean value, the standard deviation, and a 'best fit' trend line computed using a least-square linear regression." (Sensible Software, p. 29)

Managers always have a great deal of interest in identifying as much information on the costs associated

SEARCH ACTIVITY BY MONTH

YEARLY CUMULATION CSS STATISTICS
FILE   CSS   (CREATION DATE = 07/10/84)

MONTH				RELATIVE	ADJUSTED	CUM
			ABSOLUTE	FREQ	FREQ	FREQ
CATEGORY LABEL		CODE	FREQ	(PCT)	(PCT)	(PCT)
		1.	51	12.5	12.6	12.6
		2.	53	13.0	13.1	25.7
		3.	40	9.8	9.9	35.6
		4.	20	4.9	4.9	40.5
		5.	38	9.3	9.4	49.9
		6.	20	4.9	4.9	54.8
		7.	24	5.9	5.9	60.7
		8.	15	3.7	3.7	64.4
		9.	26	6.4	6.4	70.9
		10.	64	15.7	15.8	86.7
		11.	42	10.3	10.4	97.0
		12.	12	2.9	3.0	100.0
		99.	2	0.5	MISSING	100.0
		TOTAL	407	100.0	100.0	

MEAN	6.012	STD ERR	0.182	MEDIAN	5.525
MODE	10.000	STD DEV	3.664	VARIANCE	13.428
KURTOSIS	-1.497	SKEWNESS	0.078	RANGE	11.000
MINIMUM	1.000	MAXIMUM	12.000		
VALID CASES	405	MISSING CASES	2		

Fig. 1. Sample display of SPSS report

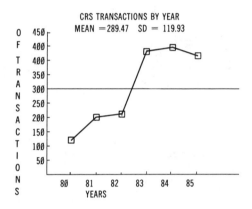

CRS TRANSACTIONS BY YEAR

YEARS	# OF TRANSACTIONS
1: 80	1: 130
2: 81	2: 206
3: 82	3: 214
4: 83	4: 399
5: 84	5: 407
6: 85	6: 379

Fig. 2. Sample display using Graphics Department's Optional Statistic Feature

with providing online services as possible. As the CSMS is designed, you can not only get the average cost of a search to the user, you can generate a report which lists these costs in a frequency order (Fig. 3).

With very little effort, you can then translate this data into a bar chart by ranging your data (Fig. 4).

If you want to look at a specific segment of your population, you can generate "subpopulation" reports. Fig. 5 shows the average cost of a search by each searcher. As you can see, for this searcher group as a whole, the average search cost for 1983-84 was $29.07. Three searchers appear to have average search costs that are not too different from each other and one searcher has a lower average search cost.

In addition, you can get a breakdown of the average costs for each user group in your total population. The subpopulation report in Fig. 6 shows for this particular online search service what the average cost per

FILE   CSS   (CREATION DATE = 07/10/84)

COST CATEGORY LEVEL	CODE	ABSOLUTE FREQ	RELATIVE FREQ (PCT)	ADJUSTED FREQ (PCT)	CUM FREQ (PCT)
	0.00	1	0.2	0.2	0.2
	2.30	1	0.2	0.2	0.5
	5.54	1	0.2	0.2	0.7
	5.60	1	0.2	0.2	1.0 1%
	6.30	1	0.2	0.2	1.2
	6.46	1	0.2	0.2	1.5
	6.89	2	0.5	0.5	2.0 2%
	7.04	1	0.2	0.2	2.2
	7.13	1	0.2	0.2	2.5
	7.16	1	0.2	0.2	2.7
	7.22	1	0.2	0.2	3.0
	7.24	1	0.2	0.2	3.2
	7.25	1	0.2	0.2	3.5
	7.31	2	0.5	0.5	4.0
	7.34	1	0.2	0.2	4.2
	7.38	2	0.5	0.5	4.7
	7.52	1	0.2	0.2	4.9
	7.67	2	0.5	0.5	5.4
	7.69	1	0.2	0.2	5.7
	7.72	1	0.2	0.2	5.9
	7.86	2	0.5	0.5	6.4 6.4%
	8.00	1	0.2	0.2	6.7

Fig. 3. Sample Display SPSS report/cost of searches

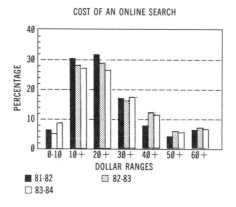

Fig. 4. Bar chart showing ranging of data

search is by user group. Although the average cost per
search for the total population is $23.47, it may be mis-
leading to quote that figure to someone requesting a
search from the business sector where the average search
cost is much higher! Similarly, this search service seems
to be providing searches at a somewhat lower-than-average
cost per search for undergraduate students.

The Crosstab report shown in Fig. 7 looks at how
search analyst activity breaks down by broad subject areas
for the year 1984-85.

Phase three of the statistical maintenance system
includes not only reporting your findings but doing an
analysis or interpretation of these findings as well.
This is where you have an opportunity to discuss trends
and emerging patterns.

Keep in mind that the analysis does not have to
be lengthy. However, without an analysis done at the unit
level, administrators are left without your insights into
what is happening in your unit. For example, in Oakland
University's Computer Search Services 1984-85 annual report, the crosstabulation table in Figure 7 is commented
on as follows:

"Appendix J illustrates the need for searchers to
be competent in many different subject areas. Twenty-
seven percent of the searches for 1984-85 were in the life
sciences. Close behind were the social sciences with
25.5% of the searches followed by education with 22% of
the searches. Business searching dropped down this year,
only picking up 16% of the searches compared to 20% from
the previous year."

As an administrator, I would be discussing this
information with the department and unit head and asking
how the unit was responding to this identified need for
its search analysts. The data is, in essence just the
catalyst to explore and look at the many factors that go
into any service unit's operations.

Any experienced online reference service coordinator knows that not all statistical information is gathered from any one source. There are many "quick and
dirty" approaches to gathering management information that
are not incorporated into the CSMS design.

You can get information from monthly vendor
billing statements that give you information on your
connect hours usage--either total connect hours of use,
connect hours use by password, or connect hours use by
database. Usually, the vendor does not produce a conven-
ient cumulative report, so you will have to use the monthly

YEARLY CUMULATION CSS STATISTICS
FILE   CSS   (CREATION DATE = 07/10/84)   – – – – – DESCRIPTION OF SUBPOPULATIONS – – – – –   07/10/84   PAGE 68

CRITERION VARIABLE COST
  BROKEN DOWN BY SEARCHER

VARIABLE	CODE	VALUE LABEL	SUM	MEAN	STD DEV	VARIANCE	N
FOR ENTIRE POPULATION			11774.3000	29.0723	18.8475	355.2268	(405)
SEARCHER	2.		2646.7700	23.4227	14.3502	205.9284	(113)
SEARCHER	3.		3115.6100	31.1561	20.5054	420.4715	(100)
SEARCHER	4.		2136.6400	30.0935	19.9697	398.7874	(71)
SEARCHER	5.		3868.2400	32.2353	19.4688	379.0329	(120)
SEARCHER	6.		7.0400	7.0400	0.0000	0.0000	(1)

TOTAL CASES =   407
MISSING CASES =   2 OR 0.5 PCT.

Fig. 5. Subpopulation report: average cost of search by searcher.

```
YEARLY CUMULATION CSS STATISTICS
FILE   CSS   (CREATION DATE = 07/10/84)                                    07/10/84              PAGE 73
- - - - - - - - - - - - - - - - - - - - - - DESCRIPTION OF SUBPOPULATIONS - - - - - - - - - - - - - - - -

CRITERION VARIABLE    COST
 BROKEN DOWN BY   USER
```

VARIABLE	CODE	VALUE LABEL	SUM	MEAN	STD DEV	VARIANCE
FOR ENTIRE POPULATION			11726.0900	29.0970	18.8673	355.9768
USER	1.	FR	8.0000	8.0000	0.0000	0.0000
USER	2.	SOPH	72.5800	14.5160	8.7757	77.0137
USER	3.	JR	130.7900	18.6843	11.3233	128.2176
USER	4.	SEN	1162.7300	21.5320	13.0671	170.7490
USER	5.	GRADM	1546.3300	24.9408	15.2377	232.1874
USER	6.	GRADP	471.7600	29.4850	23.6630	559.9382
USER	7.	FAC	6566.9600	32.9998	20.0298	401.1945
USER	8.	AP	36.6700	18.3350	6.7246	45.2200
USER	9.	STAFF	148.2100	18.5263	7.7876	60.6469
USER	10.	OTHER	116.8200	23.3640	14.7568	217.7617
USER	11.	BUS PRIV	1025.1800	37.9696	23.2657	541.2945
USER	12.	NON OU STUDENT	408.6300	25.5394	12.8498	165.1186
USER	70.		31.4300	31.4300	0.0000	0.0000

```
TOTAL CASES =    407
MISSING CASES =    4 OR 1.0 PCT.
```

Fig. 6. Subpopulation report: average search cost by user group

billing statements and add it up on your own. Try using a spreadsheet software package if you want to save yourself some calculation time.

BRS has a system-specific feature, the ACCT file that provides BRS users with cumulative data on connect hours use, but it is done on a January-December calendar year. This causes some problems for those who want to look at the data on a fiscal year basis, which ties it into their contract year. Again, use graphs to present your data, as illustrated in Figure 8 and 9.

YEARLY CUMULATION CSS STATISTICS
FILE   CSS   (CREATION DATE = 06/21/85)
- CROSSTABULATION OF -
SEARCHER   BY SUBJ   SUBJECT FIELD OF SEARCH

COUNT ROW PCT COL PCT TOT PCT	SUBJ BUS ECON ON 1.	EDUC 2.	OTH SOC SCI 3.	LIFE SCI 4.	PHYS SCI 5.	OTHER 6.	ROW TOTAL
SEARCHER							
1.	13 14.0 21.7 3.4	23 24.7 28.0 6.1	23 24.7 24.0 6.1	23 24.7 22.5 6.1	9 9.7 33.3 2.4	2 2.2 20.0 0.5	93 24.7
2.	16 31.4 26.7 4.2	5 9.8 6.1 1.3	10 19.6 10.4 2.7	19 37.3 18.6 5.0	1 2.0 3.7 0.3	0 0.0 0.0 0.0	51 13.5
3.	12 10.3 20.0 3.7	19 16.4 23.2 5.0	27 23.3 28.1 7.2	42 36.2 41.2 11.1	13 11.2 48.1 3.4	3 2.6 30.0 0.8	116 30.8
4.	3 10.7 5.0 0.8	4 14.3 4.9 1.1	11 39.3 11.5 2.9	7 25.0 6.9 1.9	2 7.1 7.4 0.5	1 3.6 10.0 0.3	28 7.4
5.	12 34.3 20.0 3.2	8 22.9 9.8 2.1	7 20.0 7.3 1.9	5 14.3 4.9 1.3	0 0.0 0.0 0.0	3 8.6 30.0 0.8	35 9.3
6.	4 7.4 6.7 1.1	23 42.6 28.0 6.1	18 33.3 18.8 4.8	6 11.1 5.9 1.6	2 3.7 7.4 0.5	1 1.9 10.0 0.3	54 14.3
COLUMN TOTAL	60 15.9	82 21.8	96 25.5	102 27.1	27 7.2	10 2.7	377 100.0

TITUS

NUMBER OF MISSING OBSERVATIONS =   2

Fig. 7. Crosstab report on search activity by subject area.

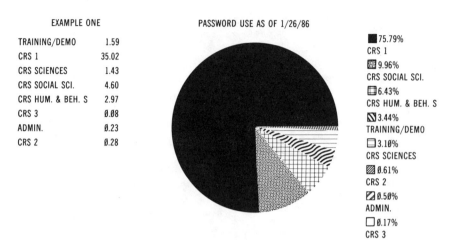

Fig. 8. Example 1 of report on connect hours use by password

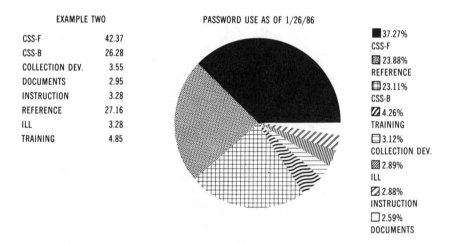

Fig. 9. Example 2 of report on connect hours use by password

In summary, I encourage all librarians to think seriously about the ways in which they can strengthen their system for maintaining online reference services statistics.

Take advantage of the new technologies which make

it easier to use computers--especially microcomputers to o
your statistics.

Take some planning time to clearly define not
only what it is that you want to count, but why you need
to count it at all.

Work on improving how you present your find-
ings--move away from just reporting numbers. Use graph-
ics--they make a difference.

Recognize that as library managers, we really do
need good information on which to base our decisions. We
should always strive toward getting the best management
information we can with a minimum amount of effort.
Systems such as the ones used at NIU and Oakland are
designed to do just this.

Whether you use any one or a combination of
computerized statistical packages that run on mainframes
or micros, spreadsheet or graphics software, or database
mamagement files, you will find one thing common to using
all of them. By getting computers to do the work, you
really will have better online reference statistics.

Bibliography

Chin, B., and Fruth, B. PFS:graph user's manual. Mountain
        View, Calif: Software Publishing Corporation, 1984

Hitchingham, E., Titus, E., and Pettengill, R. "A Survey
        of Database Use at the Reference Desk" Online 8
        (1984): 44-50.

Hitchingham, E., Titus, E., and Pettengill, R. Online
        Services at the Reference Desk (Abstract).
        Proceedings of the American Society of
        Information Sciences 19 (1982): 133-134.

Nie, N., Bent, D., and Hull, C. SPSS: Statistical Package
        for the Social Sciences. New York: McGraw-Hill,
        1970.

Norusis, M. J. SPSS: Introductory Statistics Guide. New
        York: McGraw-Hill, 1983.

Roose, T. "Search Records for Decision Making", Library
        Journal 110 (July 1985): 42-43.

Salomon, K. Computer Search Services Annual Report
        1984-1985. Rochester, Mich.: Oakland University,
        Kresge Library, 1985.

Sensible Software, Inc. Graphics Department Version 2.
        Birmingham, Mich.: Sensible Software, Inc., n.d.

Economic Trade-offs of
Information Delivery Systems

John J. Regazzi

In order to understand the future direction of the
H. W. Wilson Company's use of modern information handling
technologies, particularly CD-ROM catalogs, it is important
for me to provide you with some background regarding the
Company's automation efforts and its present electronic
publishing programs.

I have divided this paper into four major areas:
1) a very brief overview of the scope of the H. W. Wilson
publishing effort, 2) a discussion of the factors responsible for automating the Company's editorial efforts and
launching into the electronic publishing field (factors
also responsible for our interest in CD-ROM publishing),
and 3) an overview of our present electronic publishing
efforts, including Wilsonline and Wilsearch. (It is the
functional capabilities of these two efforts that will
form the basis for future CD-ROM effort.) Finally, I would
like to discuss our present plans for an optical disc
publishing program.

As we first began considering the automation of the
Company, and as we now consider the possibility of introducing a new technology such as CD-ROM, we had to address
three areas:

1. What is the need?
2. Do we have the capability to meet this need?
3. How do we respond specifically to this need?

The first and perhaps most basic question is: Why

72

change? The answer we heard when we began our automation
efforts, and which we continue to hear today, is that our
customers need and are demanding change for:

> Improved information services--print and online
> access is not enough;
>
> Expanded information services--access to one
> index or one type of information is too
> restricted;
>
> More cost effective information services--the
> need for access to electronic information
> is widespread. It is needed not only by
> businessmen and scientists, but also by
> college and high school students, and by
> public and public library patrons as well
> as by many other professionals such as
> teachers. The single greatest obstacle to
> the use of these systems by these con-
> stituencies is price.

How is it possible to improve and expand services
while reducing costs and why is it necessary to do so?
First, there have been tremendous developments in the
information technologies since the late 1960s. Second,
there is now much more information available and available
in machine readable form. For example, in 1970 a mainframe computer capable of executing 1 million micro instructions per second cost $3,000,000, or $3 per instruction. Today, using the same manufacturer, a computer
capable of executing 6.2 million micro instructions per
second costs $850,000, or 15 cents per instruction--a
savings of 95%. Similar savings of 80% for magnetic storage and 70% for telecommunications processing are also
available. Thus the cost of acquiring computer capability
has been reduced greatly and made affordable to individual
publishers. Microcomputers and CD-ROM further amplify
these cost savings and reductions. Third, more information
is available, more types of information such as numerical
data and full textual data are available, and graphic and
image information is beginning to appear. This will enable
publishers to merge different information forms together
to form new information products.
    Against this backdrop of cost reduction and
expanded services lies the haunting reality that monies,
public and private, need to be stretched further and
further for the acquisition of information. This is
particularly true for the nonprofit and voluntary sectors,
including colleges, schools, public libraries, and others.

From the perspective of the publisher, what is required to change? Does the publisher have the necessary systems expertise to launch a successful electronic publishing program?

It is no longer enough for publishers to be conversant with the content and production of their intellectual properties. Now they are being called upon to become experts in the dissemination of those properties as well. Publishers must remain in full control of their intellectual properties if they are to offer cost-effective electronic services. They cannot relinquish the decisions on what should be contained in a database, or how it should be organized.

Finally, publishers need to stay in direct and close contact with their clients. The field of publishing is changing rapidly and publishers, in order to change effectively, need to listen to their customers.

The future development of information delivery systems will depend upon three key factors:

1. Technology
2. System design
3. Economics

Does optical disc publishing meet the need of publishers and consumers? What are its benefits and disadvantages?

Benefits
    Publishers: Expansion; more value; per-unit cost reduction
    Consumer: More information; more powerful access; broader access; reduced costs.

Disadvantages
    Publishers: Deeper investment in systems; additional training and support requirements and costs; potential conflict with existing products
    Consumers: Cost of acquisition vs. payment for only information; system performance (possible degradation) additional costs of hardware and software and training.

There is a high demand for change. Publishers need

to integrate their editorial and system resources to
respond to the changing needs of electronic publishing.
And they need to stay in close contact with their clients
in order to respond to those rapidly changing needs.

Frontends and Gateways:
Financial Considerations and Uses

Joseph T. King

With the current trend toward increasing automation
in the library, many information professionals have become
inundated with products. Reeling from the effects of jargon that is at times nebulous and ambivalent, librarians
are striving to sort facts and understand what all the
high-tech hype is about.

Confusion over jargon has been the case for front-
end/gateway software. The terms "gateway software,"[1]
"gateway system,"[2] "frontend software,"[3] and "frontends" have been open to debate since the inception of the
products. This name ambivalence has led to much confusion
and disagreement. The name jumble has also been directly
related to the rapid change in emerging products, thereby
making an encapsulating term very difficult.

This name schizophrenia is just one facet of the
overwhelming push to develop products that will somehow
simplify all of the complexities associated with information gathering and dispersal. The concept of "Let Hertz
put you in the driver's seat" seems to have become more of
an anthem for the online industry than a slogan from the
sixties. The commandment "Thou shalt not take the seat of
the enduser at the computer terminal" has become a sacra-
ment in information delivery and in the philosophy of reference service.

A consensus of opinion shapes my definitions for
these products and I hope the definitions will abate
rather than augment the confusion. Frontends for personal-
computer-based online searching are software packages that
run on personal computers and allow the user both offline

selection of databases and the ability to upload and download searches for further manipulation with word processing
packages. This serves to differentiate these products
from user friendly systems and gateways. Some of the more
well known examples are Microcambridge, Pro-Search, Sci-
Mate, Searchworks, Searchware, Searchhelper, PC/Netlink,
Dialoglink, Searchmaster, Searchlit, and Wilsearch.
       Frontends can also reside on a mainframe as well,
substituting an interface with user friendly menus. These
are also known as user friendly systems. They tend to
serve the enduser in their orientation. Examples would be
BRS Brkthru, BRS Afterdark, Knowledge Index, Dialog Business Connection, BRS/Saunders Colleague, ..Menu on BRS
(which allows user friendly commands on the BRS system),
Paperchase and Mead. Gateway systems are transparent
systems that act as conduits for the user. They connect
the user to databases on other remote host search services
or they connect users to their own databases.[4] Examples
are Easynet, Inet, Iquest, and Unisen. While this list is
not exhaustive, it represents the better known products
for most users.
       Having offered these basic definitions and a
sampling of product names, I would like to cover a little
of the history of these products, give an indication of
their current uses, list some of the problems libraries
are facing in their use, discuss financial considerations,
and give some information about what characteristics are
important for personal-computer-based frontends.

ENDUSER MARKET AND PRODUCT HISTORY

       If the seventies were the decade of the inter-
mediary, then the eighties are the decade of the enduser.
Endusers are being pursued as never before, for several
reasons. There has been a great increase in online
services available and in the types of information users
can access. According to Cuadra's 1986 Directory of
Online Databases,[4] since 1979 the number of databases
has risen from 400 to 2901, the number of database
producers from 221 to 1379, the number of online services
from 59 to 454, and the number of gateways from 0 to
35.[5] The number of endusers doing their own searching
has risen dramatically. According to Wanger and Cuadra in
1976, seven percent of endusers did their own searching.[6]

In 1986, the figure has certainly risen. While no actual
figure is available, database vendors now regularly have
endusers in their initial training courses. It is also
apparent from the popularity of these products that
enduser searching is on the increase.

The primary reason for such widespread growth in
both online services and the desire to search them is the
development of the personal computer. Clinicians, scientists, educators, lawyers, and business executives can
access these services at any time in the convenience of
their offices or homes. With the emergence of such items
as the smaller and less expensive IBM-PC AT and the development of CD-ROM, we are seeing the beginning of an era
that recognizes the spending power of the enduser. Endusers have become an attractive item in the online industry because they represent virgin market territory. Most
vendors have reached a peak in marketing to intermediaries
and are looking for new markets.

The endusers themselves are interested in going
online for several reasons. First, they don't have to
make an appointment to see the librarian or searcher which
often has meant considerable time delay in the past; they
can search whenever and wherever they want. Second, they
can save money by reducing costs whether by searching at
non-prime time or paying only flat connect-hour charges.
As their access to information increases so does their
eagerness to seek out information in more sophisticated
ways. Not content to receive a mere printout of citations, many want more versatile capabilities. Some want
to download the search to disk and then utilize a file
management package for post processing of the search.
Still others want to pick up the search via electronic
mailboxes downloaded from a remote micro through an information network such as Ontyme II. Some want to form
their own searcher pools, borrowing expertise from a
variety of online searchers with subject specialization--a
sort of Group Online Practice idea, with specialists in
each area. Some even see themselves as directing a lot of
their own training.

Another reason for the enduser wanting to get online is the importance of information and the need for
quick access. Physicians need to have the very latest
information possible, sometimes in life-or-death emergency
situations and they find the personal computer a good and
reliable friend for information dispersal. As information
gains clout in a society switching from goods and commod-
ities, there will continue to be the need for efficient
systems and software to assist with searching.

PRODUCT HISTORY

The idea of attempting to bring the enduser to the computer terminal is not a new one despite the current hoopla. ISI developed the first frontend designed for endusers, called <u>Primate</u>, in 1978. The software, which was a reprint file management package, eventually was followed by <u>Sci-Mate</u>. Eager not to be outdone, each of the major vendors has in its turn come out with either a software package or user friendly system. Dialog utilized the Menlo Corporation to design <u>In-Search</u> in 1984 for microcomputers, and this was upgraded to <u>Pro-Search</u> for BRS and <u>Dialog II</u> in 1985, Dialog created its own front-end, <u>Dialoglink</u>, in 1986 while continuing <u>Knowledge Index</u>, which it started in 1982, and expanded to include <u>Dialog Business Connection</u> in 1986, SDC came out with <u>Search-master</u> in 1984, and the National Library of Medicine came out with <u>Grateful Med</u> in March of 1986. BRS created <u>BRS Afterdark</u> in 1982 and <u>Brkthru</u> in March of 1985. In 1984, <u>BRS/Saunders</u> created <u>Colleague</u>, which includes the full text of several well known medical texts online. Database producers as well as software companies have gotten into the act. <u>Wilsonline</u> produced Wilsearch in 1985. <u>Disclosure</u> came out with <u>Microdisclosure</u> in 1983 for its databases, General Informatics Corporation, which is now owned by Sterling Software, came out with <u>PC/Netlink</u> in 1983. Information Access created <u>Searchhelper</u> for its databases in October 1983. <u>Paperchase</u> is a user friendly system that used the existing tapes of the National Library of Medicine's <u>Medline</u> databases and back files to create a user friendly program designed by physicians/ computer scientists for physicians. It was created in 1979 and came out in 1981. <u>Microcambridge</u> was designed for the <u>Cambridge</u> databases and came out in 1985. Finally, Telebase Systems came out with <u>Easynet</u> in 1982 and <u>Iquest</u> in 1986, and OCLC introduced <u>Unisen</u> in 1986. There are many products in this category and this is not a comprehensive list, but an idea of the major ones.

CURRENT TRENDS AND APPLICATIONS FOR THE INTERMEDIARY AND THE ENDUSER

With the current emphasis on automation, frontends and gateway systems are finding a niche for themselves in

the library setting as well as in the home of the enduser. With continued access to more and more systems,
there is every indication that we are seeing just the tip
of the iceberg and that these products will continue to
develop and will eventually have more sophisticated functions. Information professionals must be aware of these
products for they will often be called upon to act as con-
sultants in the purchase of some products or services.

Although the functions of personal computer frontends tend to overlap in serving user groups, they primarily
serve either intermediaries as a group or endusers as a
group. The needs of each group are different.

Features that are important to the intermediary
include some of the following:

Command Language Interchange. The product
Pro-Search has been designed more for the information
professional with many features that are useful for a
librarian. For example, using Pro-Search, the librarian
who has limited knowledge of one database can search it
with another system's commands. Built into the software
is an interface to translate Dialog commands into BRS
jargon and vice versa. Sci-Mate has a built-in universal
language translator which will alter commands into the
language of the host search service. For those who only
rarely search SDC or NLM, the software will alter the
commands you enter into a structure suitable for the ORBIT
and NLM computers.

Staff Training. Frontends can be used to teach
library assistants some of the more basic routine-type
tasks associated with searches. The frontend
Search-Master allows the user a script mode which can
create a program of menus and user friendly screens for
novice users. In this way, SDI's and other routine online
work such as interlibrary loans can be handled by a
paraprofessional.

Financial Accounting. Another library task which
can be handled by frontends is library search accounts.
Procedures can be facilitated with frontends such as
Pro-Search, Dialoglink, and Searchworks, which have an
accounting feature as a part of the software. This
feature can detail search information for a given month,
including a breakdown of session reports and summary
reports by client, charging codes, searcher, database,
or online service. For libraries using manual methods,
automating this procedure can save time and money. This
feature can also eliminate the need to re-enter data into
Lotus or another spreadsheet.

Typing Ahead of Commands. Intermediaries are always anxious to reduce online time since the ticking of the clock represents dollars. With this feature, one can send a set of instructions for the computer to handle and then type ahead of the computer so that other commands can be addressed in a more immediate manner. This can be done with Pro-Search, Searchworks, and Dialoglink. One can also upload a search strategy with just about any of the frontends for personal computers, which can save time and money by eliminating lengthy typing and preventing typos. The personal computer frontends designed for the intermediary orientation include Pro-Search, PC/Netlink, Dialoglink, Searchworks, and Searchmaster.

The following features primarily serve the enduser:

Post-Processing of Citations. The reformatting of downloaded citations into either a tailored style-sheet form or a form that includes analyses or graphs is known as post processing. Post-processing of information offline at present is still rather basic. The products mentioned will work with the downloading of text into ASCII files, allowing the user to use word processing packages, and some will allow line editing after the search. However, a frontend with the ability to post-process the search into a sophisticated indexing system or information analysis report is still a new concept. In the case of Sci-Mate, the searcher works with the Manager as well as the Editor in reformatting citations for the various style sheets of journal publications, but the user has to purchase separate software. This is also true for several other frontends. Searchworks has a capacity built into the disk to reformat citations to a limited extent. It advertises a record editor and the ability to sort and index citations. As for analyzing information in some meaningful way, Microdisclosure, a frontend for the Disclosure databases, has the ability to work with a spreadsheet in order to create financial analysis reports. It can create graphs and charts which work only with the Disclosure databases. This is one area that software companies are concentrating on since so many people are interested in this capability. Future developments should be interesting.

Database Selection. This is another feature important to the enduser. This capability aids the user in choosing which database to use. At present database selection aid is limited. While database selection is considered more of an issue for endusers, librarians as well can use assistance when deciding on databases.

Pro-Search offers the user some suggestions in attempting
to analyze database selection. The user is given the
choice of several subjects arranged in a card-catalog
style. When a subject is selected, the user is directed
to several databases on the subject. The user is then
given online connect-hour costs and the emphasis of the
database. Although simple in design, sophisticated
database selection is still in the planning stages.[7]
This feature could be improved to include some type of
ranking of databases, given a certain topic, and perhaps
eventually a more sophisticated database selector. Such
help is possible to a limited degree with Searchware and
Pro-Search. Searchware offers the user a menu of 54 broad
subject categories with 10 databases per category. With
this software, the user is able to enter the Dialog
Dialindex and get the number of postings per database on a
subject before the search is executed. With Pro-Search,
the user can select a subject category and then enter
either Dialindex or Cros online and get an estimation of
postings for a subject. The user then could choose the
file which had the greatest number of documents for the
actual search. Although the user must know a subject
category and define the topic in its broadest sense, this
added feature is handy.

Of course, the various gateway systems such as
Easynet and Iquest offer database selection and search
execution as a part of the bargain, even though it is
transparent to the user. My problem with this is that the
rationale for database selection remains esoteric and is
based on the judgment of the online vendor. I believe
that the big advantage of gateway systems in database
selection is the ready updating done instantly online--the
ability to provide the user with the latest database
information due to the nature of the system's construction.
While a piece of software needs updating even before it
leaves production and reaches the consumer, this is not a
problem with gateway systems.

PRODUCT PROBLEMS

The user needs to be aware of some problems with
personal computer frontends which are not always apparent
and came to my attention after I worked with them for
awhile. The first of these is the problem of modem pools.
Many librarians in corporate environments do not have the

luxury of the individual modem. Users pool or share modems. Some of the software will not work with pooled
modems or at least will not work very well. This is
something I have not experienced as we have Hayes modems
at Norris, but it has been reported to me by corporate
librarians. The problem is due to an extra step in the
log-in protocols which is handled more easily by some of
the software. There is also a problem with updating software and difficulty in using software that is outdated
almost before it is released from the producer. There is
the problem of copyright and all the other problems one
has with software purchase such as disc protection, li-
censes, etc. There is also the problem of vendor support
and viability. I believe that the best products are not
always supported by the biggest companies and the biggest
companies do not always have the best products.

The impact of CD-ROM will certainly have an effect
on the market for these frontend products and on what
their place will eventually be. CD-ROM is revolutionizing
our current way of thinking concerning online services and
will certainly produce more significant thought as it
gains in popularity. We also have to wonder about the
quality of information accessed by the enduser and what
consequences this information will have on the delivery of
critical care, such as when physicians are making life-and-
death judgments based on the information they find. This
point was brought out very well by Bonnie Snow of Dialog
Information Services in a keynote address to the Association of College and Research Libraries' Science and Technology Section's program, "End User Searching: Issues in
Instruction, Systems Selection, and Administration," at
the 1986 ALA Conference. In her paper, Snow alluded to
the idea we information professionals must assume a certain responsibility when teaching the neophyte. When we
put the endusers in the driver's seat, are we sure they
will become good drivers or will they kill someone? This
has to be of concern.

FINANCIAL CONSIDERATIONS

With the emergence of these new products and
services into the library, there are financial considerations that one must be aware of. Some of the considerations that affect the intermediary are the following:

   Software Purchase. This includes the software
itself and any licensing agreements, as well as fees for
system updates and package upgrades as they occur. There
is also the question of whether the library wishes to act
as a purchasing agent for other departments.
   Billing Accountability. For librarians using
gateways and frontends, who will pay for these services
and how will they be billed? Will they be issued a department account or will they pay as they go? Who will pay
for paper and supplies used when searching? If there has
to be an enduser station, how will it be financed? Who
will pay for the extra micros, furniture, and supplies?
   Staff Time. Along with concern for the financial
considerations related to the actual physical product,
there also needs to be concern for the expenditure of
staff time in all or some of the following situations:
troubleshooting enduser problems with machines and/or
software, issuing passwords to users, billing users,
collecting and processing fees, dealing with searches
which result in zero retrieved hits, investigating new
programs by attending either seminars or demonstrations,
creating publicity or teaching materials, giving hands-on
demonstrations, and constructing enduser courses construction where applicable. Librarians need to become educated
in these areas, which means either sending them to classes
and workshops or budgeting staff time to attend local
online user group meetings. These types of expenditures
are difficult to estimate but have big impact.
   Conversely, staff and money saved by these products
can be significant for endusers and intermediaries alike,
and worthy of mention as a financial consideration. For
the intermediary, uploading a search which was created
offline and being able to type ahead of the host computer
reduces online time and can mean savings. Also, searching
a database such as Dialog without any prior knowledge can
create a lot of anxiety and a rather large online bill.
The intermediary who owns Pro-Search and knows BRS commands does not have to worry about such a problem. He or
she can use BRS commands to search Dialog, saving time and
worry.
   Finally, there are financial considerations which
affect the enduser more significantly and need to be
considered. The involvement of librarians can be very
important since the enduser will want to consult them when
making software purchases or when considering searching a
user friendly system. The enduser must consider how much

work can be saved by using the product and how valuable
the product is for them. Obviously the more the product
is used, the faster users will see a return on their
investment. So to a large degree, this area is an individual matter dictated by the needs and practices of the
enduser. One can point out that the enduser will save
money in connect-hour charges if he or she is using the
system more effectively. The enduser will also save a lot
of time in managing citations to post-process if he or she
owns a reprint management package or a database management
system package which works with the frontend. In the
final analysis, the question of how much this access to
information is worth to endusers is the one which will
determine how effective the product will be for them.

PRODUCT EVALUATION AND WHAT MAKES A GOOD FRONTEND

        This last section refers primarily to personal-
computer-based online frontends and is meant as a helpful
guide. Careful perusal of all the products available will
help the user determine which product to purchase. In
selecting software, the user must first list the most
important functions that the software needs to accomplish. All of the software and systems have certain key
weaknesses and strong points, depending on the user's
needs.
        A good frontend designed for a personal computer
should have certain basic functions; some of them make the
product exceptional and others are almost expected. The
more basic features would include the ability to create
the search offline, upload it, and then download the
results. The downloaded text should work with any word
processing package using an ASCII-type file. Some of the
products on the market will only work well with special
file management packages which require additional expense
if they are not already owned.
        One should look at several general factors con-
cerning software to begin with. The product should be
easy to learn, and should include a good manual and pref-
erably some sort of tutorial disk. If possible, there
should also be a demo disk available for the product.
Considering what the product is capable of should indicate
what the user should pay. The price should be competitive
with the market but not drastically higher. High price
does not always assure a good product. The product should

also be able to act as a general telecommunications package with features such as automatic log-on and autodial.

The core of the product, the user friendly interface which translates commands and changes command input, should access a variety of databases and a minimum of two. Be aware of how often the software is upgraded. Look at the company's reputation and size. Are they new in the software business? How many institutions use their product? Can the user demonstrate the product either with a free sample or at minimal cost? What hardware does the user need? What are the operating system and memory requirements for their machine? What is the vendor support like? Is it offered infrequently or on a regular basis?

The help features should be easy to call up and rather brief. If possible, such items as Dialog blue sheets should be online with the database selected. The manual for the product should be easy to read, well-indexed, and brief. Sometimes the user needs a manual to explain the user manual. Many new searchers are reduced to tears or fits of despair at the terminal because they do not even know how to open up the program. This can be serious.

If one were to shoot for the moon, the following features would be added. There would be a really sophisticated database selection capability. One would be able to ask for a very complex subject that might overlap several topics and get just the right database or databases for that subject. As we stated, this is still in the future. One would also want a really good post-processing package within the frontend software. This might include a search editor to reformat all the citations into any style sheet the user wanted, an indexing system to sort the data so that it could be retrieved by any keyword, and the ability to analyze the data into a report with graphs and statistical analyses. Finally, a model frontend would permit the user to access all the capabilities of the system and then offer some type of instruction. This is the case with Paperchase, which suggests appropriate Medical Subject Headings from the MESH thesaurus for the Medline database after the search is completed.

CONCLUSION

In conclusion, the emerging technology we see in frontends/gateway and software/gateway systems, as with

all technology in the information marketplace, is in flux
and is creating new ways to manage information dissemination. With a concrete opportunity to influence information seekers and users, the information professional is
caught in a double bind. Still reeling from last year's
video disc and this year's newest optical reader, we
service-oriented professionals want to serve our public
the best way we can, but are not sure which way that might
be. We want to keep our bases covered, but can we? With
so many products on the market and the neverending changes
in technology, we need to do our homework. The call for
us to be pioneers in a new era can be challenging and
exciting.

Notes

1. F. Spigai, "Gateway Software: A Path to the
End-User Market?" Information Today 1(1):6-8 (February
1984.

2. M. E. Williams, "Gateways: Electronic Paths to
Medical Libraries of the World," Healthcare Online
1(2):5-6 (November 1985).

3. D. T. Hawkins and L. R. Levy, "Frontend
Software for Online Database Searching. Part 1:
Definitions, System Features, and Evaluation," Online
9:30-37 (November 1985).

4. C. Cuadra, Directory of Online Databases (New
York: Cuadra/Elsevier, 1986).

5. Ibid.

6. J. Wanger, C. A. Cuadra, and M. Fishburn,
Impact of Online Retrieval Services: A Survey of the
Users, 1974-75 (Santa Monica: System Development
Corporation, 1976).

7. Hawkins and Levy, "Front End Software for
Online Database Searching." Part 1, 30-37.

Full Text Online Delivery: Economic Realities

Delores Meglio

For more than 10 years since information professionals began regularly searching online databases for information, there has been the promise of the day when simply typing in a few commands on a typewriter keyboard could draw forth the full text of virtually any information that has ever been published. We have seen parts of that vision come to reality; yet we are a long way from the limitless library of computer information that was imagined. As we all know, there are many barriers--real and imagined--to the routine gathering of full text material online. What we once saw as an orderly progression in the expanded availability of full text databases has proven not to be the case. Instead, we witness many false starts.

HARSH ECONOMIC REALITY

Economic reality is a driving force at this stage in the development of full text online services. And reality can come as a shock to the database developer as well as the user. This spring we learned that two ambitious online full text services--the videotex programs of Knight-Ridder and the Times Mirror Companies--have been abandoned. Despite investments of $50 million in one service and $40 million in the other, neither was able to attract and sustain the subscribers and use necessary to encourage continued investment in their development.

My company, Information Access Company, has an unparalleled history in the delivery of periodical full text files. We were one of the first publishers to offer full text databases of widely read general interest and business publications and we are among the few companies to offer our files on the three major information services: Mead Data Central, Dialog, and BRS. I state these facts, not as self-promotion, but to place our experience with full text in perspective. Being among the first, as Knight-Ridder and Times Mirror will vouch, enables you to learn some expensive lessons from which followers will benefit.

Full text databases generally have been created based on several suppositions. It is supposed that if the total cost of retrieving full text articles online is less than that of a print search, one would naturally opt for online. Wrong.

It is supposed that offering hard-to-find facts in a readily accessible medium would have subscribers online around-the-clock. Wrong.

In IAC's case, it was supposed that the thousands of searchers who regularly use IAC's Magazine Index and Trade & Industry Index would automatically call up the full text of relevant citations when it was available. Wrong.

As the newspaper videotex experience demonstrates, it takes a much broader leap of logic to recognize the value of online full text delivery. Theoretically, librarians, investors, businesspeople, and sociologists would have been in line for the first subscriptions to the Knight-Ridder and Times Mirror systems because, for the first time, they would be able to access city and regional news virtually as it happened. No need to wait for the copy of a newspaper to be mailed from a city across the continent, because the information it contained would be available online before print copies began hitting doorsteps and newsstands.

Perhaps more important over the long view, subscribers would be able to pull up full histories of the economic and social development of complete geographic regions. Naisbitt, in his Megatrends predictions, used just this search tactic to predict the major opportunities for the future. He and members of his staff painstakingly tracked local and regional coverage of a wide variety of economic, technological and social issues. They identified those that were on the rise by the number of column inches devoted to their coverage in local newspapers, and

predicted their demise as the column count receded. Besides keeping the user in touch with regional news throughout the country, a system such as those offered by either
Knight-Ridder or Times Mirror put this same forecasting
power into the hands of any user.

ECONOMIC VIEW NOT SHARED

You can see how the systems' developers became
mesmerized by their idea. Unfortunately, not enough
people shared their vision. With daily newspapers selling
at 50 cents or less a copy, few people could understand
why anyone would want to pay 10 times that amount to
retrieve and print out a single article or view a single
service such as the stock tables. Now that is the harsh
economic reality of full text delivery. There has to be a
widely shared perception of value for a database to become
economically viable.

IAC, with a lengthy history in online databases,
began developing full text files with somewhat more scaled-
down expectations. The overall usage of our full text
services is very close to what we projected; however, they
are being accessed infrequently by a large number of
searchers, rather than frequently, as we envisioned, by
large public, academic, and corporate libraries.

COST CURTAILS USE

In polls of users and potential users, cost--or
perceived cost--is the single greatest barrier to routine
retrieval of full text material online. That's not sur-
prising. Yet, it is not the level of cost that appears to
be the barrier, but any cost at all.

Our surveys were restricted to Dialog users alone,
because the IAC databases were not available on Mead or
BRS until early this year and the experience of subscribers to those services was not sufficient to provide a
valid survey.

Also, to put our survey into further perspective,
there has to be an understanding of the scope and coverage

of the IAC full text files. IAC offers largely retrospective material of general and business interest in its
full text databases. Our files therefore represent a
general information source for a wide range of users.
With new materials appearing approximately two weeks to a
month after publication of the magazine or journal, the
IAC databases would not have the same appeal that, for
instance, a daily updated financial file would have to
investors. Also IAC full text databases would not be as
heavily used as files dedicated to aerospace or automotive
publications by members of those industries. However, the
IAC databases provide the general information with sufficient currency to have value to virtually everyone at
some time or another.

Our studies were aimed at developing projections
for the future of our own full text files and to gain an
understanding of the future use of full text databases
generally. Obviously, it is vital to have this information in order to project future pricing and products.
One of the most revealing facts to come out of our studies
is that few libraries have calculated the cost of print
retrieval services. They have nothing against which to
measure the true cost of online retrieval. In conver-
sations with librarians who are comfortable with com-
puter-assisted searching, we continually hear about the
frustrations of accounting systems that do not reflect the
contributions that online retrieval can make to economical
library operation. Online searches show up as a cost item
on the budget, while print or microfilm searches are ab-
sorbed in payroll costs--even if these costs are two or
more times as expensive as retrieving the same material
online. Queens Borough Library in New York successfully
presented the case for online economics to its administration. Today, many requests for bibliographic reference searches at the library's Ready Reference Desk are
fulfilled online. If the needed full text is not available within the library and is accessible online, it is
retrieved. Queens Borough has demonstrated that it is
often as economical to obtain an article online as to
search out a source and get it through interlibrary loan.

The Queens Borough Library Ready Reference Desk may
be somewhat unusual in that it assures patrons of up to 40
citations--if they exist--on any topic or person. To
manually compile such a bibliography, the library has
calculated, would involve labor costs up to 10 times the
charge for an online search and printout.

PRINT SEARCHES PERCEIVED AS FREE

However, in most libraries print searches are
viewed as free while online retrieval is seen as costly.
Queens Borough does not pass along online costs to patrons
because the administration views online as a cost-effective method of providing patron services. Queens Borough
believes that charging for any service automatically
restricts its use to those who can afford it and under-
mines the library's charter to serve everyone within the
community equally.

Some libraries, such as Chicago Public and Dallas
Public, have drawn a line that is acceptable to patrons.
Online searches to support personal or student projects
are free, while research for local businesses is charged
at actual cost. Both of these libraries actively support
their local business communities and have established
business reference sections. Salt Lake County Library, in
addition to offering free online searching to all patrons,
includes free delivery of materials to patrons within a
specified radius of the library.

NO METHOD FOR ACCOMMODATING ONLINE COSTS

The economics of online searching for both
bibliographic and full text material, it appears, is in
the eyes of the beholder or more precisely in the ledger
of the library budget. Those libraries that have done
cost accounting to make the most effective use of their
human resources are those that have incorporated full text
retrieval into their reference services. Predictably, our
polls revealed that corporate librarians are making the
greatest use of full text files and account for almost
half of all activity. Companies are generally accustomed
to doing cost analysis to increase productivity and therefore can more easily equate labor-saving aids such as
online searching with more economical operation.

Even in the corporate environment, however, we
found some strong price resistance to online retrieval of
full text. Often, company libraries charge back to the
requesting department the cost of online searches while
offering print searches at no fee. When the requestor has
the option of free or fee, you can guess which is selected. On the other hand, if the search media are left
to the discretion of the librarian with no penalty to the

patron, and if online is an option, it is often the first source chosen in order to save staff time.

As I have stated, the heaviest use of full text online retrieval is among corporate librarians, and that use breaks down into three subcategories. General industrial product companies use the IAC full text files to track information on their competitors, their markets, and their industries, as well as to gather data on contemporary issues relating to personnel, management and consumer practices which affect how they do business. New among the most frequent use-per-subscriber corporate libraries are investment firms gathering data on specific companies and industries. Finally, marketing and consulting firms are regular corporate users of our full text databases.

Other libraries in order of usage of full text are the general reference departments of academic libraries, law libraries, and medical libraries both in schools and teaching hospitals. This group accounts for some 30 percent of full text accesses.

The least frequent per-subscriber-use of the full text files is among public libraries. This bears out what public libraries have told us: there is often no acceptable method of charging patrons for full text retrieval and no budget provision to accommodate increased online costs.

As a bit of background, our survey revealed that the greatest number of libraries which subscribe to Dialog use the service from two to five hours a month accessing a number of the 200 databases available. Of that time, an average of one hour is spent searching the ten IAC databases, both bibliographic and full text.

For every access of full text files, more than two searches are made of IAC bibliographic databases. Again, for background, the most heavily used IAC online database is Magazine Index, with the Computer Database a close second. Interestingly, though Magazine Index is used almost twice as frequently as Trade & Industry Index, its companion full text file, Magazine ASAP is used less frequently than Trade & Industry ASAP.

USE CONTROLS PRICING

Usage levels are the single greatest influence on the pricing of any full text database. Generally, all

development and maintenance costs remain similar whether
10 or 10,000 people are using the information. And the
costs of creating and sustaining a full text database are
significant. Despite the fact that we now have optical
character readers which, theoretically, could input articles directly from print to computer format, none of the
readers can accommodate the wide range of typefaces that
publishers use. Even obtaining typesetting tapes from the
publication does not work, because deadline corrections
and changes often are not represented in the master tape.
So, each article must be individually keyed. This is a
tremendous investment in labor. All material must then be
proofread, corrected, and matched to the appropriate
citations. These costs exist no matter how many people
use the database. Theoretically, usage beyond the break-
even point should ultimately result in reduced costs. The
reality of full text databases--at least retrospective
files--is that few developers have reached the break-even
point to test this theory. Continuing costs based on
per-use are royalty fees to the publisher of the article
and access fees for the information supplier. Less than
half of all payment for accessing a full text database,
irrespective of telecommunications charges, goes to the
database developer.

USE DETERMINES COVERAGE

     The economics of full text database development
forces the publisher to carefully watch usage. As the
cost for mounting Forbes, for instance, is the same as
that to place online a similar amount of material from a
less widely cited publication, a database publisher must
constantly look at the value of each publication based on
the frequency of users' access. Over the three years our
full text files have been available there has been an
ongoing effort to add new publications believed to be of
value to researchers. At the same time, we have discon-
tinued coverage of a number of periodicals that were receiving little or no reference. Most recently, we added 20
of the most widely read area business publications after
activity in the index files indicated that searchers had
significant interest in the contents of these magazines
and newspapers. Full text online delivery is a costly
proposition and the availability of online information
will largely be determined by the value that users place
on the databases. That value will be reflected through
usage. Even developers of not-for-profit databases are

forced to take a long, hard look at the products and to trim and expand as their subscribers dictate. Their resources, too, are finite and must be directed where they will have the most benefit.

COST--ANY COST--A BARRIER

In our surveys of our online customers, we tested the value of full text online delivery to their organizations: is an article worth $1, $10, or $100? Naturally, the interest waned as the price went higher, but there was virtually no resistance up to the point of $15 an article. What was revealed was that any charge was a barrier. For patrons who have been conditioned to believe that information delivery is free, even a dollar an article is viewed as excessive. What was also revealed was that few libraries have any provisions for offsetting outside charges with savings in staff time. Even with lower costs for online full text delivery, will the services find adequate users to make them a routine reference source?

The economic hurdle in online usage--particularly access to full text files--appears to be greater than actual cost alone. It is the inability at this point in the development of the information industry for us to place objective value on the searcher's time and skills. Our accounting systems cannot accommodate the savings in time for a skilled librarian against the hard cost of online delivery.

Even at reduced costs, online searching, particularly full text retrieval, will not become routine in our libraries until the true costs of print retrieval are realized. As our society becomes more aware of the value of information and the skills of the information professional, services which enhance information retrieval and professional productivity will increase.

The limitless library of online information we once envisioned may arrive, but perhaps not in exactly the form we predicted. It will be a gradual evolution. The online full text resources will grow in direct proportion to users' demand for them. Whether online searches for full text will ever be a routine response to patrons' reference requests remains to be seen.

Economic perceptions--the unwillingness to pay $5 for a single newspaper article when an entire issue costs 25 to 50 cents--will influence the development of future online databases. Why pay $7.50 for an online search when your local librarian can accomplish the same result in an hour or two? After all, information is free--or almost free, isn't it?

Cost, not value, continues to be the major influence in the development of full text databases. There is no question that online has become an important library service in a short period and full text delivery is assuming its own place.

As in many emerging industries, early high hopes have led to unrealistic expectations and some disappointments. Full text delivery is still evolving. We are learning just what information users find of value. Libraries are making the case for online retrieval generally, and full text specifically as an economical approach to patron service.

That virtually limitless full text online library may have been too optimistic. We may have to settle at least temporarily for something less ambitious. Commitment, patience, and deep pockets alone--as Knight-Ridder and Times Mirror learned--cannot make it happen. Only the user's perception of value can.

We recently conducted a test to see if lowered costs would build much broader usage. We offered what we believed to be the first half-price sale of online full text data. The offer was made to all Dialog subscribers and the event was publicized in that service's mailing as well as in the online industry press. The results from the first month of the half-price offer indicated that access to full-text files almost doubled: however, full text print-off only increased 30 percent, suggesting that once a source was found, many users chose to look elsewhere for the full text of the material. Extending the sale for an additional two months did not increase usage beyond the levels of the first two months. This indicates that the half-price offering did not build sufficient new usage to suggest that there is a direct parallel between price and use of full text online delivery. The special offer encouraged access to the full text databases to see what was there, but did not significantly increase requests to view or print off the full text of articles. In fact, the results raised more questions than they answered. Did the people who accessed the files continue logging on throughout the full three months? Did the result indicate that new users came on infrequently throughout the period? Will these people continue to use the file now that pricing is back to normal? I do not have the answers. Perhaps you do. If so, I would like to hear some of them.

What Does It All Mean?

James H. Sweetland

In the early days of online searching, a major
issue was cost. In fact, the earliest RASD Machine-Assist-
Reference Section program (in Detroit, 1977) was on the
fee vs. free issue. However, today we are addressing
management issues--how can we best use our resources, how
can we maximize efficiency with quality in searching, how
can we account for what we do. In short, the fee/free
issue is finally dying its long-deserved death.

I say long-deserved because it has always been a
false issue. As Robert Heinlein has put it: "TANSTAAFL"
(There ain't no such thing as a free lunch"). No information is free--the issue is really who pays for it, and
how. Since the middle of the nineteenth century, this
country has been developing a system of libraries based on
the idea of "collective good": everyone in the community
pays a little bit (through taxes, tuition, or what have
you) for the service, and then can use it as they need it
without paying for use at the time. This principle is
used to pay for fire and police protection, schools, and
many similar public services in addition to libraries.

At the same time, we have some direct user charges
for other public services--for example, photocopying,
special holds, municipal swimming pools, and parking
meters.

If we have other direct user fees, even in libraries, and yet accept the idea of general "taxation" for the
good of all, why did fee/free become such a major issue,
particularly with online services? While the definitive
answer may be elusive, the following factors are certainly
involved in this issue:

97

First. Online is a new service. Thus, it was not in existing budgets. Nor, in many cases, was there even a clear budget line in which to put it (Is it "outside service," "computer rental," "dataprocessing," or "contractual service"?). In other words, it was wholly new, and thus very visible.

Second. The service involves outside vendors who send monthly bills in great detail. Thus, without thinking about it, library managers (and their governing bodies) can know exactly—to the penny and the thousandth of an hour, what their charges are. So, the assignment of costs for this new service was very easy.

Third. The service is customized. An online search is aimed at one user for one time. Once a search is completed, it is unlikely that the user or the searcher will ever again use exactly the same strategy or want the same results. In other words, unlike most library services, this is a "private good." And, of course, it is very easy to identify the user.

Fourth. Public funds for information and educational services began to dry up at about the same time online systems became popular. Thus, this new service competed not only with other new services, but also with all traditional services.

The result is actually amusing if you look at it correctly. Few have asked exactly how much a midweek story hour costs per user—given the time used by the storyteller, by other staff, and perhaps with overtime, by the janitor—let alone amortizing the children's media collection, the furniture in the children's room, and so on. Thus, few ask whether tax money should be used to "subsidize" a service used by a very few, or even want to know the real cost. Besides, storytelling is a "traditional" service of libraries (actually less than a hundred years old).

We are finally beginning to accept machine-aided reference as legitimate (and perhaps someday, as traditional" as story hours). Whether we charge the users directly, charge all the institution's clients indirectly, or, as is most common, do both, we are on the way to accepting the service as a legitimate part of what we do.

So, where are we going now? While predictions are always dangerous, I believe the following trends are likely over the next few years.

First, there will be Easier User Access. Gateways and frontends (and many of the optical disk systems) permit users to use automated systems without really knowing what they are doing. This has been the traditional approach to the card catalog and the printed indexes--anyone who can read, and has a little patience, can find something. Of course, you still need much more knowledge and skill to make the system work well.

Such a situation increases the emphasis on the librarian's role as teacher/consultant. Not only will the average user need to know a little about using the "user-friendly" system, but the more sophisticated user will realize the limits of both the system and his/her ability. So, the librarian will get the harder questions, and people will take the advice more seriously.

This situation, of course, will probably make the librarian's work harder, in much the way that many bibliographic instruction programs only eliminate the easy questions and increase the number of hard ones: instead of "What does 'il' mean in Reader's Guide?" we get "Which indexing service is most appropriate for this question?" and we are starting to get "Would it be more cost-effective for me to search systems A and B, or to have an intermediary search them and system C, and what other database/systems are there of value besides A, B, and C?"

Another consequence of making access to automated systems easier could be easier funding. After all, if computerized databases can be accessed by anyone, and they are readily available, what is the difference between, say, Dialindex or Wilsearch and Social Science Citation Index or even Reader's Guide? Once the machine-based systems do not appear to be so esoteric, the odds of getting general funding from the taxpayers increase.

To continue the money theme--the emotions of the fee/free issue will probably dissipate when the user has a choice. If you want to do it yourself, you can do it at home, or use a simple system at the library. If you want a better quality or more comprehensive search, you can pay for it (at the library or elsewhere). This puts machine-aided systems in the same category as, for example, genealogy--do it yourself for free, taking a lot of time and probably making errors, or hire it to be done. Part of the resistance to fees in the online environment has been the lack of choice--once it's there, many of the gut-level objections should go away.

A second major trend for the near future is Optical Disk Technology. We already see the CD-ROM and the beginnings of the WORM (write once, read memory) and, with Infotrac, the large disk. It was only a year ago that there were three vendors with prototype systems exhibiting at

ALA; depending on how you count, in 1986 there were over two dozen such systems.

The optical disk restores the traditional library role, yet does it with the latest technology. Once you have the equipment (analogous, for example, to an index table) you then buy the disk (analogous to the book or serial). You have full control over the information, in a semi-portable form, in your library. And since you are buying information in a semi-permanent form, the disks, at least, can come right from the general materials budget.

With this technology, the cost issue reverts to the traditional one--is this item in scope can we afford it, etc. The cost is a one-time cost; the cost-per-use de-creases with each use, just as it does with traditional print and audiovisual sources.

Another traditional cost issue reappears, and this one may be less positive. Since each disk system is rough-ly equivalent to one print database, the library will tend to purchase only those most used. If in the process it also drops use of remote online systems, it will lose the ability to access all those databases it does not use of-ten. It would be a real step backward if, thanks to the newest technology, the smaller library again decided it could not afford, say, Chemical Abstracts (on disk), and refused to make it accessible via online vendors.

Another effect of the laser disk is to eliminate a number of disadvantages of remote online systems. First, by scattering copies of the database all over the place, the danger of censorship is lessened. Just a couple of years ago it was seriously proposed that, since Index Medicus was now online, all references to articles based on fraudulent research should be removed from it. The author of this suggestion noted that such action would have been nice before, but was not feasible due to the number of copies of the printed index around. If we have numbers of copies of the machine-readable index we will eliminate the chance this version of 1984 will take place.

Another advantage of the inhouse system over the remote system is communications. With some experience, I have been able to predict the weather in the Rockies, based on the communications problems in getting to Dialog and SDC in California. With your own disk player, you do not have to worry about thunderstorms interfering with the microwaves or flooding out your own phone lines. And you do not have to worry about increases in long distance rates or whether your new discount phone system will go out of business in a couple of years.

A third important fact in the machine-readable world is the Expert System, or Artificial Intelligence. Such systems already exist, and do a fairly good job of playing chess, teaching Japanese to speak English, or doing simple medical diagnosis. It will not be long before they are involved in at least some kinds of information retrieval as well. I see two effects on our work from these, in addition to all those I have previously noted under "easy access."

First, as business people and physicians use AI in their own work, both they and their clients will become more used to the idea of machines as information handlers. Thus, the average library user, over time, will not only become less resistant to machines, but will also want to see them in the library.

Second, AI may finally give us the "point of use" instruction we have talked about so much in library instruction. We all know users are most likely to learn when they see an immediate payoff and when they have an immediate need. Imagine the user, never having fully understood a periodical index, sitting down at the automated version of one and getting a more-or-less personalized instructional session precisely when needed.

But there is another side to all of this. The final results could tend either to eliminate librarians nearly entirely, or at least reduce our status; or they could make us more visibly important as the only profession which deals with information as such.

First, the bad news--expert systems in some fashion could nearly eliminate librarians, at least the "generalist" reference librarian. If the expert system can answer simple questions and help find answers to more complicated ones, why should anyone go to a librarian? After all, if I need really in-depth information, I should go to a subject expert anyway. We already see many ads in the computer magazines telling users to sign up with one or another gateway system, in part precisely to avoid the librarian--who still, it seems, retains the old image of forbidding petty bureaucrat.

If this happens, the library may find itself in a very strange role, like the early public hospital or the county poorhouse--it's the low-service, least-common-denominator place for those who lack the skill, the money, or the power to get good information. In essence, the information function of the library is part of the general welfare system, but not something people really want to use.

If that projection is too dreary, how about this?
Modern technology permits information seekers to stay in
their offices or their homes, or to use what we call
"information brokers." There is really no need for a
collective "library," except for those who want some cheap
recreational reading, and for a few antiquarians who like
to browse through the book warehouse. If this happens,
the library will still get a lot of support, at almost the
opposite pole from that noted above. The library becomes,
in a sense, a rich person's toy, catering to a very limited
crowd.

Frankly, I do not like either of the above projections, nor do I think they are realistic--at least not in
light of what I know is going on in many libraries.

We know from many studies that, given the choice,
people prefer going to other people for help and for information before they go to an institution or a machine.
Thus, all things being equal, even our sophisticated information user will tend to want to see a person, regardless of how fancy the artificial intelligence becomes.

Keeping this in mind, consider the role machines
can take in labor-intensive activities like libraries.
They can be used to eliminate the drudgery and the routine
work, leaving time for people to do those things people
alone can do. Think of how much time reference librarians
could have to work with users who have more complicated
information requests if someone (or, in this context,
something) could show people how to use the card catalog,
interpret Social Sciences Index, or direct people to the
drinking fountain.

Besides freeing up our time, machines can improve
both our image and our true role. The high-tech library
looks more impressive than the one without technology. On
the simplest level, people who enter data into computers
get paid better than those who enter data into card catalogs via typewriters.

But the reality is much more important that this
image. As information handling machines become more
common, we continue to confront the problem addressed by a
MARS program of a few years ago--"Terminal Dis-Ease"--or
as Alvin Toffler called it, Future Shock. The sophisticated information user in many ways needs more help than
the unsophisticated one, and knows he/she needs it. A
user who has tried four or five databases on three different systems will realize just what can be done and what
can't. The librarian as "advisor" (or, if you prefer,
"consultant") becomes an important part of this person's

life. If we are prepared to offer value judgments, to
recommend the best database, or system, or approach, or
all of the above and then some, we will at last seize the
authority that is ours, and that we can rightfully claim
as handlers of information.

Of course, this latter projection assumes we are
going to make a real effort to keep on the cutting edge of
information handling--be it laserdisks, systems analysis,
or the special advantages of little-known databases in
arcane fields. If we claim to offer real advice, we are
going to have to take responsibility for mistakes, just as
other fields ranging from law and medicine to transmission
repair do now.

There are ways to improve what we do, whether by
looking at our operations as a whole information system,
or using technology in new ways. We know what to do, at
least in general outline. We have gone beyond concern for
the apparent costs and awe at the machine-as-machine. We
accept the computer as another information tool; now all
we have to do is figure out the best ways to use it.

Appendixes

A. Online Reference Services: Funding Methods

Created by members of the Costs & Financing Committee of RASD/MARS, June, 1984, and revised June 1986.

From the moment online information was recognized as a valuable or indispensable research aid for the library, librarians confronted the question of how to pay for this service. Availability of the service requires that funds be allocated to pay for equipment, for the training of staff, for the documentation in support of searching, and for the actual cost of the searches charged to the library by the database vendor. The nature of the costs, and an estimation of their value, are identified and discussed in a complementary pamphlet, created by the Costs and Financing Committee of MARS, entitled Online Reference Services: Costs and Budgets. This pamphlet, however, is devoted to questions of funding an online search service, and, specifically, philosophical issues in the funding of this service, practical methods of funding, and case studies of funding methods.

PHILOSOPHICAL ISSUES OF FUNDING ONLINE SERVICES

The question of payment for online information retrieval in the library takes on an ethical dimension; many librarians have felt an obligation not to charge for any services. Such charges tend to discriminate against

patrons less able to afford the cost of those services,
and thus may create a class of information-poor who
receive less service than those who can afford to pay.

The other side of the argument is that library
patrons have always had to pay for some services, including photocopying and nominal fees for borrowing materials
through interlibrary loan. It is therefore neither incon-
sistent nor unethical to charge for so specialized a service as the searching of online databases. Moreover, it
is argued that the service would not be possible at all if
libraries were not able to pass on the charges incurred
for these searches to their patrons.

A closely related issue to the question of payment
for online information retrieval is the distinction
imposed by libraries among different categories of users,
and the different rates charged them for this service.
For example, the full cost of searching online databases
may be charged to patrons not affiliated with a university,
while patrons enrolled in the university curriculum may
enjoy the service at a rate that is subsidized in part or
wholly by the university.

The debate is unresolved. To further acquaint you
with the issues of that debate, and some of the turns
which they have taken, a bibliography of items that address the philosophical issues of funding online searching
is presented below.

Blake, F. M. and Perlmutter, E. L. "The Rush to User Fees:
    Alternate Proposals," LJ, 102:2005-2008. October
    1, 1977.
Budd, John. "The Terminal and the Terminus: The Prospect
    of Free Online Bibliographic Searching," RQ,
    21:373-378. Summer, 1982.
Cogswell, John A. "Online Search Services: Implications
    for Libraries and Library Users," College and
    Research Libraries, 39:275-280. July, 1978.
Cooper, Michael D. "Charging Users for Library Service,"
    Information Processing and Management, 14:419-427.
    June, 1978.
Ensore, P. "The Expanding Use of Computers in Reference
    Service," RQ, 21:365-372. Summer, 1982.
Firschein, Oscar; Roger K. Summit and Colin K. Mick.
    "Planning for On-Line Search in the Public
    Library," Special Libraries, 69:255-260. July,
    1978.
Huston, Mary M. "Fee or Free: The Effect of Charging on
    Information Demand." LJ, 104:1811-1814. September
    15, 1979.

Linford, John. "To Charge or Not to Charge: A Rationale,"
     LJ, 102:2009-2010. October 1, 1977.
Waters, Richard L., and Victor Frank Kralisz. "Financing
     the Electronic Library: Models and Options,"
     Drexel Library Quarterly, 17:107-120. Fall, 1981.

PRACTICAL METHODS OF FUNDING

Discussion of the practical methods of funding an
online search service is difficult because aspects of an
online search service will change over time, including the
funding needs and methods of the service. Changes in
funding arise from a number of factors, including: changing service goals, changes in the external economic environment, and evolving search service needs. The two types
of costs for an online search service, i.e., startup costs
and ongoing costs, described in greater detail in the Costs
and Budgets pamphlet referred to earlier, differ in nature
and amount. Start-up costs are fixed and non-recurring.
Ongoing costs are less predictable than start-up costs.
These differences suggest different approaches to funding
at each stage of the service development. In addition,
the different methods of funding, which are outlined below, are not mutually exclusive. Typically, these methods
are used in combination, and frequently the proportion
supported by each component changes over time.
     A review of the literature of funding methods for
online searching reveals the multiplicity of approaches to
funding. Libraries often seek external sources of funding
for start-up costs and internal sources for ongoing services. The funding sources most frequently referred to in
the literature are:

I. New money
     A. Requesting new and ongoing funds from
          budgeting agency.
     B. Obtaining funds from outside sources,
          including state library agencies, Federal
          agencies, private donors and foundations.
          (Typically, these are one-time, fixed fund
          sources.)
II. Reallocation of existing funds
     A. Using money from existing library budget,
          e.g., transfer of funds from service or
          material budgets to pay for the search
          service.

B. Reallocation of funds from other units within the organization, e.g., academic departments or laboratories.

C. Implicit reallocation in the form of staff time allocated to search service, including professional librarians and clerical or accounting staff.

D. Reallocation of intangible resources for overhead, space and the like.

III. Charging end-users for searches

A. Full cost-recovery from the user, i.e., no institutional support for staff or overhead.

B. Partial cost recovery, for those parts not covered by reallocation or new money.

The decisions concerning which combination of funding approaches is best suited to an individual library can be made only at the local level where service goals and funding realities can be matched. For that reason, methods which work well in one context for one library might be inappropriate for use in another library. Case studies may suggest models or patterns helpful in a particular library setting. The select bibliography which follows is provided to aid in the identification of successful methods of funding an online search service.

Budd, John. "The Terminal and the Terminus: The Prospect of Free Online 73-378. Summer, 1982.

Drinan, Helen. "Financial Management of Online Services--A How-To Guide." ONLINE, 3:4:14-21. October, 1979.

Evans, John E. "Methods of Funding." Online Searching Technique and Management, ed. by James J. Maloney. Chicago: ALA, 1983. pp. 135-148.

Firschein, O.; R. K. Summit, and C. K. Mick. "Use of Online Bibliographic Searching in Public Libraries: A Retrospective Evaluation." Online Review, 2:1:41-55. March, 1978.

Lynch, Mary Jo. Financing Online Search Services in Publicly Supported Libraries: The Report of an ALA Survey. Chicago: ALA, 1981.

Waters, Richard L. and Victor F. Kralisz. "Financing the Electronic Library: Models and Options." Drexel Library Quarterly, 17:4:107-120. Fall, 1981.

CASE STUDIES OF FUNDING METHODS

        Funding methods for online information retrieval
have the potential of having as much variety as the number
of institutions which offer the service.   Case studies
afford insight into a variety of methods and are useful
for investigating what method has been applied
successfully in a given type of institution. While a case
study may not be entirely useful for your consideration,
isolated ideas from several studies may be able to provide
the reader with enough information to formulate funding
options or alternatives for their own institution. For
that reason, the following items are provided as a select
bibliography on case studies of funding methods for online
database searching.

Allen, David Y., ed. The Implementation of Data Base
        Searching at Three Campuses of the State University
        of New York. Based on papers presented at the
        Annual Conference of the State University of New
        York Librarians' Association (Farmingdale, NY, June
        5, 1980). p. 29 ED 198834 (Eric Document).
Crawford, P. J., and J. A. Thompson. "Free Online
        Searching in a Public Library: An Unscientific
        Study." ONLINE, 7:2:12-19. March, 1983.
Drinan, Helen. "Financial Management of Online
        Services--A How-to Guide." ONLINE, 3:4:14-21.
        October, 1979.
Hoover, Ryan E. "Computer Aided Reference Services in the
        Academic Library." ONLINE, 3:4:28-41. October 1979.
Knapp, S. D. and C. J. Schmidt. "Budgeting To Provide
        Computer-Based Reference Services: A Case Study."
        Journal of Academic Librarianship, 5:1:9-13.
        March, 1979.
Lee, Joanne H., and Arthur H. Miller, Jr. "Introducing
        Online Database Searching in the Small Academic
        Library: A Model for Service without Charge to
        Undergraduates." Journal of Academic
        Librarianship, 7:1:14-21. March, 1981.
Raedeke, Amy. "Machine Assisted Reference Service in a
        Public Library: A One Month Test Period." ONLINE,
        2:4:56-59. October, 1978.
Rouse, S. H. "Charging Policies for On-line Services in
        the Big Ten Universities." In: User Fees: A
        Practical Perspective. Littleton, CO: Libraries
        Unlimited: 1981. pp. 97-107.

B. Online Reference Services:
Costs and Budgets

Created by the members of the Costs and Financing Comittee
of RASD/MARS, December, 1983, and revised June 1986.

COST ELEMENTS

      The cost elements outlined below serve as
guidelines for budget configuration. The costs involved
in online searching can be divided into direct and
indirect categories.

      Direct costs are the costs incurred by an online
search session: the connect time charge for using a
vendor and database, the charge for the use of a telecommunications network or other telephone line, and the
charges for citations, whether displayed online or printed
offline. Search preparation and execution may be calcu
lated and itemized under direct costs or may be included
under the indirect cost of personnel—labor.

      Indirect costs include all other expenses involved
in running an online reference service. Acquisitions
covers direct purchases to be made, here divided into
equipment (even if leased), documentation and supplies.
Maintenance contracts for equipment should also be listed
as a budget item. Documentation and supplies must be
purchased. System manuals, database thesauri, and other
user aids will compose the search service's own reference
collection, together with system newsletters and
subscriptions to relevant journals. If the equipment

includes a printer,paper will be needed; if the printer is
an impact type, new ribbons will be needed.

A variety of recurring cost elements constitute the
category of operating expenses; the heading should not be
taken to imply that the costs categorized as "direct" and
"acquisitions" do not reoccur. The indirect recurring
cost elements include four general areas--personnel, training, promotion, and overhead--whose specific line items
may vary. For example, searcher and coordinator may be one
and the same person, or coordination may consume a quarter
of a department head's time. Training sessions may take
place onsite, or may require travel and overnight lodging.
Promotion may include newsletters, brochures, or complementary searches; the facility may need modification, etc.

A.   Direct
     1. Search sessions
         a. connect time
         b. telecommunications
         c. citation charges
         d. labor (searcher's time)
B.   Indirect
     1. Acquisitions
         a. equipment
             1) terminal
             2) modem
             3) telephone
             4) maintenance contracts
         b. documentation & supplies
             1) manuals
             2) thesauri
             3) subscriptions
             4) terminal paper, ribbons
     2. Operating expenses
         a. Personnel--labor
             1) coordinator-administrator
             2) librarian-searcher(s)
             3) clerical-support staff
         b. Training expenses
             1) vendor training
             2) database, subject seminars
             3) practice time online
             4) travel expenses
             5) professional memberships
         c. Promotion
             1) printing and graphics
             2) online demos, complementary searches

    d. Overhead
        1) facility use & modification
        2) furniture
  3. Utilities

SAMPLE INITIAL BUDGETS

     Some estimated cost figures are offered in two
sample budgets on page 114 intended to cover preparatory
costs and operating expenses for three months. The MARS
Costs and Financing Committee has compiled the cost
information on which these figures are based.
     The scope of Service A can be described as modest
and relatively low-cost, projecting forty searches in the
three month period, or three to four per week, in a
limited group of databases on one system. Service B is
more ambitious, has more capital, and plans eighty
searches throughout one system in the period defined.
     Search Service A purchases a 300 baud thermal print-
ing terminal with acoustic coupler and installs a phone.
No other modifications are made to the facility. Documentation and supplies include three rolls of terminal paper,
a search system manual, ten system database descriptions,
and one journal subscription. Personnel costs are based
on the estimated labor hours required of one professional
searcher-coordinator and one paraprofessional support
staff to provide this level of service. Neither staff
member is dedicated full time to the service. The searcher-coordinator attends an introductory system training
session, incurring some travel expense, and is budgeted
$50 for online practice to supplement the training course.
Promotion takes the form of a locally-produced flyer and
five strategically planned demonstrations. Search session
costs are estimated for forty twenty-minute searches at an
average connect-hour price of $50, with telecommunications
at $7 per hour and thirty citations per search at an aver-
age of $.15 each. Total initial budget: $3,139.
     Service B purchases a 1200 baud CRT or a microcompu-
ter with modem and printer. A telephone is installed and
$2,000 budgeted to modify an alcove into a search station.
Along with terminal paper and inked ribbons, funds are
provided to purchase a system manual, thirty database
descriptions, and seven primary thesauri. Two journal
subscriptions are established. The personnel budget of
Service B covers the labor costs of one searcher-coordinator, two searchers, spending two to four hours per week

in search activities with the assistance of one support
staff. Introductory system training including online
practice is held onsite (shared with another institution);
funds for additional practice time are also set aside.
Promotion involves a printed brochure and ten online
demonstrations. While planning to access only one search
system, no database restrictions are planned for the six
to seven projected searches per week. The average connect
cost used here is slightly higher at $60 per hour. A cita-
tion charge averages $.20. Total initial budget: $11,911.

The cost estimates provided here are realistic, but
the budgets should be viewed as exemplary models rather
than definitive structures. Not only do actual dollar

SAMPLE INITIAL BUDGETS: Cost estimates as of June, 1985.
Estimates to cover a three-month,
start-up period.

	Service A		Service B	
		Total		Total
Preparatory Costs				
Equipment				
terminal & modem	$ 695	$	$ 3,072	$
telephone	240		640	
maintenance contracts	30	965	87	3,799
Facility				
modificiation	0		1,400	
furniture	0		500	
utilities	45	45	100	2,000
Documentation, supplies				
paper, ribbons	9		30	
manual & thesauri	48		460	
subscriptions	78	135	148	638
Operating Expenses				
Personnel--labor				
coord.-administrator	500		620	
Libn-searcher(s)	0		688	
support staff	120	670	306	1,614
Training expenses				
system training	70		600	
practice time	50		100	
travel expenses	100	270	0	700
Promotion				
printing, graphics	40		400	
demos, free searches	125	165	520	920
Search sessions				
connect time	666		1,600	
telecommunications	93		160	
citation charges	180	939	480	2,240
TOTAL INITIAL BUDGET		$ 3,139		$11,911

figures vary, but the cost elements to be included will
depend on a multitude of decisions about the scope and
structure of the service to be provided. Additionally,
the budget itself can be arranged in any number of ways;
many other models can be found in published articles and
case studies, some of which are listed in the bibliography.

Bibliography

Chen, Ching-Chih and Susanna Schweizer. Online
    Bibliographic Searching: A Learning Manual. New
    York: Neal-Schuman, 1981. pp. 147-158.
Drinan, Helen. "Financial Management of Online
    Services--A How To Guide," ONLINE, 3:4:14-21.
    October, 1979.
Fenichel, Carol H., and Thomas H. Hogan. "Costs and
    Charging Policies," Online Searching: A Primer.
    Marlton, NJ: Learned Information, 1984. pp. 77-93.
Grimes, Nancy E. "Costs, Budgets, and Financial
    Management," Online Searching Technique and
    Management, ed. by James J. Maloney. Chicago:
    American Library Association, 1983. pp 123-134.
Hawkins, Donald T. "Management of an Online Information
    Retrieval Service," The Library and Information
    Manager's Guide to Online Services, ed. by Ryan E.
    Hoover. White Plains, NY: Knowledge Industry
    Publications, 1980. pp. 111-114.
Knapp, Sara D., and James Schmidt. "Budgeting To Provide
    a Computer-based Reference Service: A Case Study,"
    Journal of Academic Librarianship, 5:1:9-13. March,
    1979.
Matzek, Dick, and Scott Smith. "Online Searching in the
    Small College Library--the Economics and the
    Results," ONLINE, 6:2:21-29. March, 1982.
McClure, Charles R. "A Planning Primer for Online
    Reference Service in a Public Library," ONLINE,
    4:2:57-65. April, 1980.
Mount, Ellis, ed. "Planning for Online Search Services in
    Sci-Tech Libraries," Science and Technology
    Libraries, 1:1. Fall, 1980.
The Online Micro-Software Guide & Directory 1983-1984.
    Weston, CT, Online Inc., 1982.

Reynolds, Dennis. Library Automation: Issues and
       Applications. New York and London: Bowker, 1985.
       pp. 565-581.
Saffady, William. "The Economics of Online Bibliographic
       Searching: Costs and Cost Justification," Library
       & Technology Reports, 15:588+. Sept/Oct 1979.
Shirley, Sherrilynne. "A Survey of Computer Search
       Service Costs in the Academic Health Sciences
       Library," Bulletin of the Medical Library
       Association, 66:4:390-396. October, 1978.

Contributors

Verl A. Anderson is the online reference librarian, Eastern Oregon State College Library in La Grande.

Deborah L. Graham is the director of library services, Sacred Heart General Hospital in Eugene, Oregon.

Martin Kesselman is information services librarian, Library of Science and Medicine, Rutgers University, New Brunswick, New Jersey.

Joseph T. King is information specialist, Norris Medical Library, University of Southern California, Los Angeles.

Rebecca Kroll is public service librarian, Science and Engineering Library, Northwestern University, Evanston, Illinois.

James J. Maloney is marketing representative for Dialog Information Services, Inc., Palo Alto, California.

Delores Meglio is vice president, editorial services and computer operations, Information Access Company, Belmont, California.

Brian Nielsen is head of reference and coordinator of sponsored research, Northwestern University Library, Evanston, Illinois.

G. Margaret Porter is coordinator of database services for the University of Notre Dame Libraries, Notre Dame, Indiana.

Barbara Quint is editor of Database End-User.

John J. Regazzi is vice president, the H. W. Wilson Company, the Bronx, New York.

James H. Sweetland is assistant professor, School of Library and Information Sciences, University of Wisconsin, Milwaukee.

Elizabeth A. Titus is assistant director for public services, Northern Illinois University, DeKalb.